P9-CER-968

CHICKEN
FROM MARYLAND TO KIEV

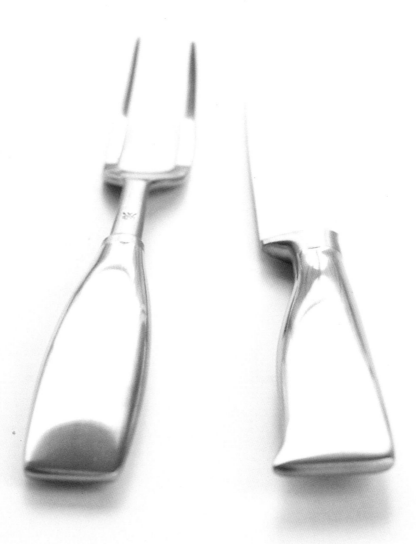

CHICKEN

FROM MARYLAND TO KIEV

CLARE FERGUSON with photography by **PETER CASSIDY**

RYLAND
PETERS
& SMALL

LONDON NEW YORK

Senior Designers Steve Painter, Sally Powell
Commissioning Editor Elsa Petersen-Schepelern
Editors Maddalena Bastianelli, Helene De Rade Campbell
Indexer Hilary Bird
Production Patricia Harrington
Art Director Gabriella Le Grazie
Publishing Director Alison Starling

Food Stylist Clare Ferguson
Assistant Food Stylist Bethany Heald
Stylist Wei Tang
Photographer's Assistant Rachel Tomlinson

First published in the USA in 2001
by Ryland Peters & Small Inc.,
519 Broadway, 5th Floor,
New York, NY 10012
www.rylandpeters.com

Text © Clare Ferguson 2001
Design and photographs
© Ryland Peters & Small 2001

Printed and bound in China

The author's moral rights have been asserted. All rights
reserved. No part of this publication may be reproduced, stored
in a retrieval system, or transmitted in any form or by any means,
electronic, mechanical, photocopying, or otherwise, without the
prior permission of the publisher.

10 9 8 7 6 5 4 3 2 1

ISBN 1 84172 163 8

DEDICATION
To my parents whose devotion to honest food, good cooking,
and excellent conviviality meant that Rhode Island Reds, White
Leghorns, and clucking bantam hens had as much right to our
garden as everyone else.
And to Ian, my husband, with love and gratitude.

AUTHOR'S ACKNOWLEDGMENTS
My warmest thanks to Bethany Heald, my deputy food stylist and
editorial assistant, and to Berit Vinegrad for her invaluable advice.
Thanks also to Christine Boodle of Better Read for her word skills.
My thanks to David Lidgate of C. Lidgate, Butchers and
Charcutiers, of Holland Park, to Haydon and Phillip of Kingsland,
the Edwardian Butchers, to the three good halal butchers, all in
Portobello Road, Notting Hill, and to Jeanne Silbert.
I am also indebted to my agents Fiona Lindsay and Linda Shanks
of Limelight Management.
Although I am grateful for the advice, opinions and expertise of
those mentioned, any imperfections in these pages must be my
responsibility, not theirs.

NOTES
All spoon measurements are level unless otherwise specified.
Fresh herbs are used in this book unless otherwise stated. If using
dried herbs, halve the quantity given.
Uncooked or partly cooked eggs should not be served to the very
old or frail, the very young, or to pregnant women.
Ovens should be preheated to the specified temperature. Recipes
in this book were tested with a convection oven.
If using a regular oven, increase the cooking times according to
the manufacturer's instructions.

contents

Introduction

Chicken is the world's favorite meat and superb recipes for chicken can be found in almost every culture. Imagine a bustling Japanese noodle bars with chicken tucked into noodles in a fragrant broth, while, snug in some remote Scottish Highland croft, there's a great black pot—with the fragrance of herbs, chicken, and leeks—hanging over a slow fire.

On the canals of Bangkok, women jockey their narrow boats, seeking to sell you their scented, coconutty chicken and shrimp soup or green curry—outrageously tempting—while in an elegant restaurant in Lyons, chicken, burgundy, mushrooms, and baby onions seethe in a gleaming copper casserole. Jump to Mexico City—we are in a traditional *refugio* where tasty chunks of chicken are being rolled up inside warm tortillas and bathed in guacamole with cheese and fresh herbs.

But these are just the start! Visit a New York downtown deli to see plates of Chicken in the Pot vanishing at the speed of light. Or visit the South Pacific and savor breast of chicken smoking delightfully over aromatics in a wok or being grilled over local brushwood at a summer beach barbecue in Australia or New Zealand.

In the hands of enthusiasts, chicken can be a revelation. In Northern India, chicken in a golden sauce spiced with exotics may be rich with almonds, cream, and butter. In North Africa, cinnamon-scented chicken is found in a glamorous phyllo-pastry crust, called *b'stilla*, and also in its world-famous speciality, the chicken tagine. In China, we can find chopsticks and bowls of wontons, stir-fries, and crispy Hunan chicken. And, in Europe, imagine a chicken pie, rich with mushroom sauce, and teenagers squabbling over crispy bits of pastry.

These creations are a tiny foretaste of the quick and easy chicken recipes in this book. Expect no hugely orthodox recipes burdened by earnest scholarly authenticity. Adapting, simplifying, or substituting has been common practice for centuries. Often the actual origins of a dish are blurred, with several countries claiming the credit. All that really counts is that the food tastes wonderful.

These chicken recipes are delicious, often fascinating, and usually very achievable. Use them for everyday meals, snacks, parties, and for easy, outdoor entertaining.

The **Americas**

The chicken dishes of the Americas have had a huge influence on the
way the world eats. You can have a chicken burger for lunch in Delhi,
grab a tortilla-wrapped chicken snack in a Copenhagen sandwich bar,
or buy Southern Fried Chicken in its many forms (from Kentucky to
Maryland) as a takeout family dinner in Sydney.

Rumaki: Bacon and Chicken Liver Kabobs

Hawaii has a lively, cosmopolitan, constantly evolving, multicultural cuisine. This easy but sophisticated snack shows Japanese and Chinese influences combined with a European touch and typical Polynesian style: it exploits the different cooking styles to excellent effect.

3 tablespoons dark soy sauce
2 tablespoons sake or dry sherry
1 tablespoon brown sugar
2 teaspoons ground ginger
8 oz. chicken livers, trimmed
8 slices bacon, halved
about 6 oz. canned water chestnuts, drained and sliced
8 scallions, trimmed and quartered

16 wooden skewers or medium satay sticks, soaked in water for at least 30 minutes

SERVES 4

Mix the soy sauce, sake or sherry, sugar, and ginger in a large, shallow glass or china dish. Using kitchen shears, cut the livers into 16 equal pieces and discard any discolored areas.

Push one end of a piece of bacon onto a soaked skewer or satay stick. Add a piece of liver, 2 water chestnuts, both at once (take care that they don't split), and some scallion pieces set crosswise. Pull the bacon lengthwise, stretching it tightly around the pieces on the skewer or satay stick and securing it back again at the first end so that it neatly encloses the entire rumaki contents in a little package. (Slide the whole little package to one end if it makes it easier.) Set the completed rumaki in the marinade and turn to coat. Continue until all 16 are made. Marinate for at least 10 minutes, then turn and marinate for another 10 minutes. (Alternatively, marinate for 8 hours in the refrigerator.)

Preheat a broiler or outdoor grill until very hot. If using a broiler, cover the tray with oiled foil. Cook the rumaki 4 inches from the heat for 4–6 minutes on each side or until they are deep, dark brown. Pour over the extra marinade as they are turned. Serve hot.

Note: If only sliced canned water chestnuts are available, use 3–4 slices per skewer. Keep prepared livers in the freezer, defrost them in the refrigerator, then use for this stylish recipe: make sure they are fully thawed before cooking.

Muffaletta is a giant, ridiculously generous sandwich which originates in New Orleans, but shows up in other areas too —try it when you're absolutely ravenous. Usually, you'll find fillings such as mozzarella, tomato, olives, lettuce, onion, ham, salami or mortadella, and often chicken, but go ahead and vary the other ingredients to your own taste.

Hot Chicken Muffaletta

4 very large, flat buns

2 tablespoons butter

7 oz. fresh mozzarella cheese, sliced

1 cup cherry tomatoes, halved

½ cup sun-dried tomato paste

8–12 small, crisp lettuce leaves

a large handful of arugula or watercress

1 red onion, sliced in thin rings

4 slices prosciutto

8 slices chorizo or salami

12 oz. freshly cooked chicken (still warm), pulled into strips

4 teaspoons Dijon mustard (optional)

¼ cup mayonnaise

SERVES 4

Cut the buns in half and spread with butter. Add the mozzarella, tomato, sun-dried tomato paste, lettuce, arugula or watercress, onion rings, prosciutto, chorizo or salami, and then the strips of warm chicken.

Dot with mustard (or spread the other half of the bun with it). Add blobs of mayonnaise. Put the top of the bun in place and press closed. Serve immediately, either whole, which is traditional, cut into quarters, or wrapped in wax paper.

Jewish Penicillin (Chicken Soup)

Perhaps the most famous of all chicken soups, this is familiarly known as

"Jewish Penicillin" and is said to cure all known ills. It is infinitely cheering,

so do go to the effort of making it now and then. Use a whole bird, cut up

(page 136), or just the wings and backs, which are rich in the gelatin that gives

this soup its body. The result can also be used whenever chicken stock is needed

for a recipe. Traditionally, a boiling fowl was used, but this is now difficult

to buy other than from gourmet or kosher butchers.

step-by-step
Jewish Penicillin (Chicken Soup)

2 lb. chicken pieces, such as backs and wings, chopped

1 onion, quartered

1 carrot, quartered

1 celery stalk, quartered

2 garlic cloves, crushed but whole

1 fresh bouquet garni (a bunch of herbs such as thyme, bay, and parsley, tied with twine)

2 teaspoons black peppercorns

salt

TO SERVE (OPTIONAL)

8 oz. shredded cooked chicken

¼ cup chopped fresh flat-leaf parsley and/or dill

other ingredients such as matzoh balls (shown), lokshen (egg noodles), rice, or tiny pasta such as stellete

MAKES 2 QUARTS, SERVES 4

1 Put all the ingredients except the salt into a large saucepan or Dutch oven with 2 quarts cold water. Bring to a boil.

2 Skim off and discard the foam that rises to the surface. Reduce the heat to a simmer. Partially cover and cook for 1½–2 hours. Add salt to taste.

3 Pour through a strainer. For a clearer stock, line the strainer with wet cheesecloth or wet paper towels (straining this way will take a long time). Remove the flesh from the bones, shred it, and reserve, covered. Discard the skin and bones.

4 To remove fat from the stock, let the stock cool a little, then trail torn paper towel edges across the surface. Alternatively, chill the stock (preferably overnight), then remove the thin film of solidified fat with a spoon.

5 Return the stock to a clean saucepan, add the shredded chicken, bring to a boil, and reheat. (The soup can be served this way, without any additional accompaniments.)

6 Serve the soup with matzoh balls or lokshen, chopped herbs and your choice of other ingredients (see variations, below). Lokshen should also be cooked in boiling salted water until done, then added to the soup in the same way.

Note: To make matzoh balls, put ½ cup medium matzoh meal in a bowl with 1 beaten egg, 2 tablespoons warm water, and ½ teaspoon salt. Stir well, then chill in the refrigerator for 20 minutes to firm up. Wet your hands, take pieces of dough the size of a marble, and roll into balls. You should have about 16–24. Poach them in a large pan of boiling salted water for 5 minutes. Remove with a slotted spoon, put on a plate, cover, and set aside. To serve, reheat in the salted water, drain, then add to the hot soup. For lighter balls, use 2 eggs instead of one—whisk the yolks and whites separately, stir in the yolks into the matzoh meal and salt, then fold in the beaten whites.

Variations

• Add ¼ cup rice, broken vermicelli, farfalle, or tiny star pasta (stellete). Cook until the rice or pasta is tender. Serve topped with chopped fresh parsley.

• Add 1 oz. dried porcini, morels, or other dried mushrooms to the hot, strained stock. Cook for another 20 minutes, adding the cooked chicken after 15 minutes. Add 4 tablespoons dry sherry or Madeira and a handful of chopped chives, then serve.

• Blanch a handful each of finely sliced carrot, celery, and leek or scallion in boiling water, then add to the hot soup 5 minutes before serving. Add sprigs of fresh chervil or tarragon and serve.

5

6

Chicken Fajitas

In Spanish, *fajita* means "little belt." In food terms, it is a strip of skirt steak marinated in a chile-based mixture before cooking. For chicken-lovers, the same marinade sparks up the flavor of the bird beautifully. This Tex-Mex classic, whether beef or chicken, is rolled up in a flour tortilla together with your choice of accompaniments.

To make the fajitas, mix the lime juice, garlic, chiles, and annatto or corn oil in a shallow glass or china dish. Add the chicken, turn to coat, and marinate for 2 hours or overnight in the refrigerator. When ready to serve, sauté or char-grill for 3–4 minutes or until done.

Put the beans in their sauce into a bowl and mash with a fork to make a coarse purée. Spoon into a bowl. Season to taste.

Scoop the avocado flesh into a bowl, add the lime juice, and mash well. Stir in the arugula and salt. Put the sour cream, if using, and grated cheese into 2 separate bowls.

Warm the tortillas in a covered steamer, on a heatproof plate set over boiling water, or in a microwave in short, 10-second bursts. Wrap in a cloth.

To eat, each guest should assemble their own tortillas by adding a line of bean purée, a layer of chicken, the avocado, sour cream, and cheese. Roll up and eat with the fingers: messy but good.

Southern Fried Chicken appears in many guises, according to the state from which it comes. Some are deep-fried, some sautéed; some dipped in flour, some in batter, some in breadcrumbs. We all know the famous version from Kentucky, while Chicken Maryland is deservedly a classic. Maryland, often breadcrumbed, is served with accompaniments such as cornbread, fried bananas, and gravy.

Southern Fried Chicken

To make the coating, put the flour, salt, pepper, paprika, seasoning mix or celery salt, and sugar in a plastic bag. Seal the bag and shake well. Add the chicken pieces, 3–4 at a time, to the bag of flour mixture and toss to coat. Arrange the pieces on a tray and continue until all are coated. Chill, uncovered, in the refrigerator for 20 minutes.

Assemble a wire rack in a roasting pan and put in a preheated oven at 350°F. Put the oil into a deep-fryer or heavy, straight-sided saucepan and heat to 350°F. To test, add one small section of chicken: it should sizzle immediately.

Fry in batches of 5–6, adding the pieces one at a time, using tongs. Fry for 8–10 minutes or until each is golden and crusty. Remove and drain on crumpled paper towels until all the batches are done. Make sure you return the oil to the correct temperature between each addition. Transfer all the chicken to the wire rack in the preheated oven and roast for a further 20 minutes until cooked through. (Cut open a piece to check: it should not be pink near the bone.)

If making Cream Gravy, heat the oil in a saucepan and stir in the flour until bubbling but not browned. Gradually stir in the milk, add salt to taste, then cook until thick and creamy.

Serve hot, with the gravy and wedges of lemon or lime, if using.

Variation
Chicken Maryland
Dip the chicken in ⅔ cup all-purpose flour, then into 3 eggs beaten with 3 tablespoons milk, then into ⅔ cup dried breadcrumbs. Chill for 20 minutes, then cook as above.

3 lb. chicken pieces, evenly sized, soaked in ice water for 20 minutes, then drained and patted dry with paper towels

lemon or lime wedges, to serve (optional)

6 cups peanut or olive oil, for frying

COATING MIX

1½ cups all-purpose flour

1½ teaspoons salt

1 teaspoon ground white pepper

2 teaspoons paprika (hot or mild)

2 teaspoons chicken seasoning mix or celery salt

2 teaspoons superfine sugar

CREAM GRAVY (OPTIONAL)

3 tablespoons of the frying oil

3 tablespoons all-purpose flour

1 cup whole milk

salt, to taste

SERVES 6

Jamaican Jerk Chicken

All over Jamaica, there are jerk huts or stalls set up on beaches, near bars, on street corners, and by bus stations. Tourists and locals alike enjoy jerk chicken or pork. Locals often use prepared spice mixes, though many take pride in creating their own jerk mix. This one is my favorite.

3 lb. chicken pieces

JERK SPICE MIX

2 tablespoons ground allspice

2 tablespoons ground ginger

2 tablespoons dried thyme

2 tablespoons dried onion flakes

2 teaspoons salt

juice of 2 lemons

2 teaspoons cayenne pepper or 1 habañero chile, seeded and finely sliced

2 tablespoons brown sugar

6 garlic cloves, crushed

4 scallions, finely chopped

2 teaspoons sweet paprika

2 tablespoons dark rum

2 tablespoons peanut or corn oil

TO SERVE

2 limes, halved

1 scallion, sliced

SERVES 4

To make the Spice Mix, put all the ingredients in a food processor and blend to a sticky paste.

To prepare the chicken, prick the pieces all over with a sharp knife. Put the Spice Mix into a plastic bag. Add the chicken and seal the top. Shake the bag until the pieces are well coated. Marinate in the refrigerator for at least 2 hours or overnight. Remove the chicken from the bag.

Prepare an outdoor grill with one side higher and hotter than the other. Cook the chicken over the hotter area, fleshier side down, for 4–5 minutes, then turn and repeat the process.

Move the chicken to the cooler part of the grill. Cook for a further 10–15 minutes, turning as necessary. Do not let the pieces char. Serve with halved limes and sliced scallion. Suitable accompaniments include a fresh salsa of tomato, cilantro, and chile, plus soft, fresh bread rolls, flatbreads, or rotis.

Variation
Cook, uncovered, in a preheated oven at 375°F for 35–40 minutes or until browned and cooked right through.

Chicken Pot Pie

Chicken pie comes in many guises, from Chicken Pot Pie in North America to *B'stilla* in the Middle East. They all feature a single or double crust of golden pastry—flaky, shortcrust, phyllo, biscuit dough, or puff pastry as here. To save time, buy it ready-rolled if possible, otherwise buy a block and roll it out yourself.

1½ lb. boneless chicken thighs and breasts, halved

1 cup chicken stock or milk

½ cup light cream or half-and-half

6 celery stalks, chopped

2 leeks, cut into ½-inch pieces and well washed

8 oz. new potatoes, halved crosswise

4 garlic cloves, chopped

1 lb. cooked ham, cut into 1-inch cubes

4 tablespoons salted butter

6 tablespoons all-purpose flour

½ teaspoon freshly grated nutmeg

¼ cup chopped fresh flat-leaf parsley

salt and freshly ground black pepper

1 package frozen puff pastry dough, 1.1 lb., defrosted

1 egg yolk, beaten with 1 tablespoon milk, for glazing

5-cup pie dish, 3 inches deep

SERVES 6

Put the chicken, stock or milk, cream, celery, leeks, potatoes, garlic, and ham into a large saucepan. Bring to a boil, reduce the heat, cover, and simmer for 20–25 minutes or until the chicken is tender.

Pour the pan contents into a colander set over a large heatproof measuring cup—there should be about 2 cups of liquid. Discard any extra or make up the quantity using a little extra cream or milk.

Clean and dry the pan, add the butter, and melt gently over a moderate heat. Stir in the flour until bubbling, but do not let the mixture start to brown. Add the hot poaching liquid, about a third at a time, heating and stirring well between additions, until the mixture is thick, smooth and velvety. Stir in the nutmeg and parsley, then add salt and pepper to taste. Add the contents of the colander and toss gently in the sauce until well coated. Cool for 10 minutes.

Roll out the dough to about ¼ inch thick and at least 2 inches bigger than the pie dish. Put the dish upside down on the dough and cut around it, leaving a 1¼-inch border. Cut a ¾-inch wide strip of dough to fit around the edge of the dish. Brush the edge of the dish with water and stick the dough strip on top. Ladle the filling into the dish, piling it up high in the center.

Wet the dough strip. Set the dough lid on top and press into place. If there is any excess, trim it off evenly. Cut a ½-inch vent in the center, then brush glaze over the top of the pie. Mark decorative patterns in the dough, if preferred, or leave plain.

Bake towards the top of a preheated oven at 425°F for 25 minutes or until the pastry is puffed, then reduce to 400°F and cook for a further 15 minutes or until the top is crusty and golden. If it browns too quickly, cover it with a folded sheet of wetted parchment paper. Serve hot, straight from the dish.

Europe

Chicken, in European cooking, has always taken pride of place and featured in many of its greatest celebration dishes. French classics, such as *Poule au Pot* or *Coq au Vin*, are still dinner party favorites, while restaurants around the world proudly offer dishes like the Russian Chicken Kiev or the French *Poulet à la Crème*. Special family meals all over Europe often include a perfect, succulent, golden, roasted chicken as a hallmark of excellence—Parsley Chicken in Denmark or Sunday Roasted Chicken in Britain. However, now that chicken is no longer expensive, it has become an everyday ingredient, rather than one that appears only on special occasions.

This midsummer fare is adapted from a dish I enjoyed at 192, our favorite wine-bar-restaurant in London's Kensington: its inspiration is, I am sure, from Spain. You can buy a whole chunk of chorizo sausage—or a string of smaller ones—to slice yourself. Most good gourmet stores stock chorizo (mild or spicy), and many supermarkets do too.

Warm Chicken and Chorizo Salad

Heat a nonstick skillet or stove-top grill pan, add the chorizo slices or chunks, and sauté gently on all sides until the juices run and the edges are slightly crisp. Set aside.

Mix the vinaigrette ingredients together in a small bowl or pitcher. Use some of the mixture to brush the zucchini halves, then add them to the still-hot pan and cook for 5 minutes on each side or until hot and golden.

Put the chicken into a large salad bowl and add the lettuce leaves and olives. Drizzle over the remaining vinaigrette, then add the chorizo and its juices, and the cilantro or parsley. Toss well, then serve immediately with garlic bread, toasted ciabatta, or warmed focaccia.

3 mild or spicy chorizo sausages, about 4 oz., cut crosswise into coin-shaped slices, or a 6 oz. piece, cut into chunks

12–16 baby zucchini, halved lengthwise, about 10 oz.

1 lb. boneless, skinless, cooked or smoked chicken, cut or pulled into long strips

4 cups loosely packed mixed red and green lettuce leaves

½ bunch arugula or watercress

16–20 black olives, about 3 oz.

sprigs of cilantro or flat-leaf parsley

VINAIGRETTE

2 tablespoons balsamic vinegar

⅓ cup extra virgin olive oil

2 garlic cloves, crushed

kosher salt or sea salt and freshly ground black pepper

SERVES 4

Cock-a-Leekie

Cock-a-leekie is a Scottish classic, consisting mainly of chicken wings, giblets, and barley—an easy, economical "big soup" meal. In the past, in the small stone crofts (farm cottages), a whole chicken and its broth would bubble deliciously in a cauldron hung in the open fireplace. Prunes add extra sweetness—but a spoonful of brown sugar could do instead.

1 lb. large chicken wings

8 oz. chicken giblets, excluding liver, or extra wings

8 oz. stewing beef

1½ lb. leeks, well washed, whites cut into ½-inch slices, green parts finely shredded

a small bunch of fresh thyme, tied with twine

a few parsley stalks, plus 4 tablespoons chopped leaves, to serve

2 tablespoons pearl barley, about 1 oz.

2 onions, quartered

2 large potatoes, quartered

12 pitted prunes or 1 tablespoon brown sugar

kosher salt or sea salt and freshly ground black pepper

SERVES 4

Put the wings, giblets, beef, white of the leeks, thyme, parsley stalks, pearl barley, and onions in a large saucepan and add 2 quarts boiling water.

Bring to a boil, reduce the heat, cover, and simmer over a moderate heat for 50 minutes to 1 hour. For the last 15–20 minutes, add the potato pieces, prunes or brown sugar, and finely shredded green parts of the leeks, and cook until the potatoes are done.

Using tongs and a slotted spoon, carefully take the beef out of the saucepan and put it on a plate. Cut the beef into 4 pieces and return them to the soup. Taste and adjust the seasoning.

Ladle the soup into large bowls, sprinkle with the chopped parsley, and serve accompanied by crusty bread rolls.

Variation
If you prefer, you may omit the beef altogether, but adjust the seasonings carefully to balance the flavors.

My mother-in-law taught me the recipe for this simple, semi-smooth pâté. Excellent for snacks, party appetizers, or picnics, the whole pâté can be made in under 10 minutes. It can be eaten warm, but is usually better cooled and chilled—I use the freezer for speed. Decorate the butter seal with some peppercorns and extra sprigs of thyme.

Chicken Liver Pâté

1½ sticks salted butter, cubed

12 oz. chicken livers, trimmed and halved

¼ cup brandy

2 garlic cloves, crushed

1 onion, chopped

½ teaspoon kosher salt or sea salt flakes

¼ teaspoon freshly ground nutmeg

2–3 tablespoons fresh thyme leaves

TO SERVE

sprigs of thyme

about 20 peppercorns

SERVES 6–8

Heat ½ stick of the butter in a nonstick skillet. Add the livers and sauté over a high heat for 2 minutes, stirring constantly. Standing well back, carefully add the brandy and light it with a match. Let flame for 1–2 minutes, shaking the skillet, then add the garlic, onion, salt, and nutmeg and cook for a further 2 minutes until the liquid has almost all evaporated and the livers and onion are golden. (Ideally, the livers should still be pink inside.)

Add the thyme and another ½ stick of the butter and heat until the butter has melted.

Transfer the mixture to a food processor. Blend, in 4–5 short bursts, to a semi-smooth paste. Spoon into 1 large or 4 small china pots. Smooth the surface. Melt the remaining butter. Pour it over the surface, adding a decorative topping of thyme and peppercorns, pushing them into the butter.

Let cool, then put for at least 1 hour in the freezer. Transfer to the refrigerator and chill for 1–2 hours until very cold and firm. Serve the same day with Melba toast or crisp, toasted slices of baguette, or store longer: flavors improve for up to 1 week.

step-by-step

Chicken Liver Risotto

This is the classic method for making Italian risotto, with hot stock added ladleful-by-ladleful, letting it be absorbed between additions. I also use an easier, more workaday version: you add the stock all at once, cover the pan, and let it simmer for 18–22 minutes. It may not be traditional, but risotto can be as elegant or as basic as you like. There are versions of this dish all around the world—add paprika, allspice, thyme, cayenne, diced bell pepper, and some spicy sausage, and you have the famous Creole "dirty rice."

Chicken Liver Risotto

2 tablespoons extra virgin olive oil

2 tablespoons salted butter

8 oz. chicken livers, trimmed and halved

8 oz. mushrooms, sliced

1 onion, sliced

1½ cups arborio or carnaroli risotto rice

2½ cups boiling chicken stock

½ teaspoon kosher salt or sea salt flakes

½ cup sweet white vermouth

a bunch of chives, cut into 2-inch lengths or chopped

SERVES 4

1 Heat the oil and butter in a preheated, heavy sauté pan. Add the chicken livers and mushrooms and sauté for 2 minutes. Remove the livers and mushrooms from the pan with a slotted spoon. Put them on a plate and set aside.

2 Add the sliced onion and sauté for 2 minutes.

3 Add the rice and stir with a wooden spoon until all the grains are well coated with oil and start to become translucent around the edges, about 2 minutes.

4 Add the salt and one-third of the hot stock and bring to a boil. Simmer until the liquid has been absorbed, then repeat, adding a ladle of stock at a time, stirring, until all the liquid has been used and the rice is tender but still *al dente* in the middle—about 6–7 minutes each time.

5 Return the livers and mushrooms to the pan on top of the rice. Drizzle over the vermouth. Cover and cook on a low heat, undisturbed, for 3 minutes. The risotto should be soft but soupy and the livers hot. Taste and adjust the seasoning.

6 Serve in heated dishes, sprinkled with chives.

Variations

• At the same time as the vermouth, stir in ⅔ cup seedless raisins and 2 crushed garlic cloves.

• Substitute 7 oz. sliced or cubed raw chicken for the livers and mushrooms. Return to the pan with the last ladle of stock. Serve topped with flat-leaf parsley.

• Chop 4 slices pancetta (Italian bacon), speck (cured ham), or cooked ham and add to the risotto at the same time as the livers or chicken.

• Substitute Madeira or dry Marsala for the vermouth.

Poulet à la Crème

This traditional, famous dish comes from Normandy, which is legendary for its cream and dairy products. A classic sauté, it seems luxurious, yet the ingredients are modest, hardly outrageous at all. Calvados (apple brandy), mustard, cream, cider, and apples combine in a voluptuous sauce. Use a quality chicken for this dish, perhaps a corn-fed or organic bird. A great party dish for relaxed entertaining.

Heat the butter and oil in a large, flameproof casserole or sauté pan. Add the chicken and sauté until well browned. Standing well back, carefully add 2 tablespoons of the Calvados and light it with a match. Shake the pan over the heat for 2–3 minutes. When the flames die down, remove the chicken pieces using a slotted spoon. Set aside in the oven to keep warm.

Add the garlic to the pan, stir, then add the mustard, cider, half the tarragon, salt, and pepper. Reserve ¼ cup of the cream and stir the rest into the pan. Return the chicken to the pan, bring to a boil, reduce the heat, cover, and simmer for 25 minutes.

Add the apple wedges and cook for a further 10–15 minutes, or until tender. Discard the tarragon. Transfer the chicken and apple to a serving dish and keep hot in the oven.

Put the egg yolks in a small bowl and stir in the remaining cream and Calvados. Add ¼ cup of the hot sauce to the bowl and mix well. Stir the egg mixture into the pan. Cook very gently, swirling the pan and its contents gently or stirring until the sauce becomes thickened and velvety. Taste and adjust the seasoning, then pour the sauce over the apple and chicken. Sprinkle with the remaining fresh tarragon and serve.

about 2 tablespoons unsalted butter

2 tablespoons extra virgin olive oil

3 lb. chicken, cut into 12 pieces, or 2 lb. boneless chicken breasts, halved crosswise

3 tablespoons Calvados (apple brandy) or brandy, warmed slightly in a ladle or small saucepan

4 garlic cloves, crushed

2 tablespoons Dijon mustard

1 cup hard cider

leaves from a small bunch of tarragon

1 cup light cream or sour cream

2 crisp apples, such as Golden Delicious or Granny Smith, peeled, cored, and cut into wedges

2 egg yolks

kosher salt or sea salt and freshly ground black pepper

SERVES 4–6

French Roasted Chicken

In France, cooks might choose a *poulet de Bresse* or *Label Rouge*—both fine birds which have enjoyed an enviable outdoor lifestyle and consequently have marvelous flavor. If you have a V-shaped poultry rack, cook the bird breast down in the French manner. Otherwise, use any appropriate rack which will hold the bird firmly, when set breast down. No rack at all? Set the bird first on one side of its breast, then the other, then breast up for the final stage.

2½–3 lb. free-range or organic chicken

2 tablespoons unsalted butter

4 garlic cloves, well crushed, plus 4 whole heads of garlic

6 tablespoons robust red wine, such as Cabernet Sauvignon, Shiraz (Syrah), or Pinot Noir

kosher salt or sea salt and freshly ground black pepper

melted butter or olive oil, for brushing

SERVES 4

Put the butter and crushed garlic in a small bowl and blend well. Push some of the mixture under the breast skin and leg skin. Skewer the neck skin closed underneath. Season the bird all over with salt and pepper. Slice the tops of the whole heads of garlic, if using, cutting them part-way through, and brush them all over with melted butter or olive oil. Set aside.

Preheat the oven to 425°F. If using a roasting rack, set the bird breast down on the rack in a roasting pan. Roast for 45 minutes, then add the whole garlic heads, reduce the heat to 375°F and roast for a further 30 minutes.

To test the chicken, pierce the thigh in the thickest part using a skewer. The juices should run clear and golden. If the juices still look at all pink, cook a little longer.

Transfer the chicken, breast up, to a serving dish, add the whole roasted garlic, if using, and put in the dish in the oven. Turn off the heat and leave the door slightly open. Set the roasting pan on top of the stove over a high heat and stir in the wine, scraping up all the sediment from the bottom of the pan. Boil down until syrupy. Serve this unthickened juice—the French call it *jus*—with the roasted chicken. The sweet, soft, roasted garlic should be squeezed out of the papery coatings and eaten with the chicken.

Note: If you wish to remove the wishbone, as the French do, before cooking, work the skin of the chicken loose over the breast and thighs with your fingers. Wiggle the wishbone free and cut it out, trying not to puncture the skin. This will make it easier to carve when cooked.

Poule au Pot

The story of *Poule au Pot* is one of the world's most famous food legends. In 1664, Henry IV, King of France, promised that, if God would grant him longer life, he would make sure that all the peasants in his kingdom would be able to afford to have chicken in the pot every Sunday. It is one of the great classic recipes of French *cuisine bourgeoise* and of chicken dishes in general.

Season the chicken well and put the butter inside. Wrap the bacon over the breast and loosely truss the bird with twine (page 138). Put it in a large casserole, breast up, then tuck in the bouquet garni, cabbage, carrot chunks, and onions. Add the peppercorns and salt.

Add boiling chicken stock or water to cover and return to a boil. Skim off any foam, and skim from time to time during cooking. Reduce the heat to a simmer and cook gently for 1 hour, either on top of the stove or in the oven, preheated to 300°F. Add the remaining vegetables, return to a boil, and continue simmering for a further 30 minutes, or until all the vegetables are tender.

If making the Cream Sauce, blend the arrowroot, cream, salt, and pepper in a small saucepan, add ⅔ cup of the hot cooking stock and bring to a boil, stirring, over a medium heat. Stir until thickened. Remove the bacon from the chicken breast and chop it finely. Add it to the sauce, then stir in the chopped fresh parsley. Transfer to a gravy boat.

When ready to serve, transfer the chicken to a large serving platter (use large serving spoons and take care or the bird will fall apart). Arrange a selection of the vegetables around the bird. Pour some of the cooking stock into a small pitcher.

Serve the platter of chicken with the pitcher of stock and Cream Sauce.

Note: Traditionally, *Poule au Pot* provided 2 courses. The cooking stock was served first as a soup, with a few chopped herbs scattered over the top, followed by the chicken, sauce, and vegetables as an entrée.

3½ lb. chicken, preferably free-range

2 tablespoons butter

8 slices bacon

1 fresh bouquet garni (a bunch of fresh mixed herbs, such as thyme, parsley, bay leaf, and celery, tied up with twine)

½ Savoy cabbage, halved and tied up with twine

1 large carrot, cut into large chunks, and 4 medium carrots, left whole

4 whole onions, stuck with 2 cloves each

2 tablespoons black peppercorns

2 teaspoons salt

boiling chicken stock or water, to cover

other vegetables, to taste, such as small whole leeks, small turnips, or small parsnips

CREAM SAUCE (OPTIONAL)

2 tablespoons arrowroot

¼ cup light cream

1 tablespoon finely chopped fresh flat-leaf parsley

salt and freshly ground black pepper

SERVES 4–6

Coq au Vin

This version of the traditional French *Coq au Vin* is a brasserie special and, in fact, a classic sauté. Use a superb chicken with a really good red wine and the dish can be sublime. Cooking the onions and mushrooms at the start streamlines things later. (Nothing could be worse than overcooking them by stewing for the whole cooking time.)

¼ cup extra virgin olive oil

16 baby onions, peeled

12 button mushrooms

4 oz. bacon lardons (strips) or 4 slices bacon, cut into small pieces

3½ lb. chicken, preferably free-range or organic, cut into 12 pieces

2 tablespoons all-purpose flour

1 teaspoon kosher salt or sea salt and freshly ground black pepper

a small bunch of fresh thyme

1½ cups red wine, such as Cabernet Sauvignon or Shiraz (Syrah)

1 cup chicken stock

2 garlic cloves, crushed

a small bunch of fresh flat-leaf parsley, chopped

croutons, to serve (optional)

SERVES 4

Put half the oil into a large, ovenproof casserole and heat well. Add the onions and sauté, stirring, for about 5–6 minutes until well browned. Add the mushrooms. Cook for about 2–3 minutes more. Transfer the onions and mushrooms to a plate and reserve.

Add the remaining oil and lardons or bacon to the pan, sauté until the fat runs and the lardons or bacon slices turn golden-brown, then remove with a slotted spoon and add to the plate of onions and mushrooms. Dust the chicken pieces with flour, salt, and pepper. Brown, in 2 batches, for about 4 minutes on each side.

Return all the chicken to the pan, then add the bacon, thyme, wine, stock, and garlic. Bring to a boil, reduce to a simmer, cover the pan, and cook for 25 minutes, undisturbed, or until the chicken is fairly tender. Add the mushrooms and onions for the last 5–10 minutes.

Using a slotted spoon, transfer all the solids to a serving dish and keep hot. Boil down the cooking liquid over high heat until a little syrupy. Pour the liquid over the chicken, sprinkle with parsley, and serve.

Note: Traditionalists would add heart- or diamond-shaped croutons of bread. Sauté them until crisp in a mixture of virgin olive oil and butter.

For centuries, in many parts of the world, chickens have been wrapped in wet clay and cooked in the embers. This is a modern refinement: a clay pot or snug casserole takes the place of the clay and an ordinary oven takes the place of the embers. The method accentuates fine flavors, so choose a really good bird. Don't panic at the amount of garlic: it will cook to a mild, subtle creaminess, while adding saffron gives a gilded, luxurious effect. Unglazed clay casseroles must be treated with care, so follow the manufacturer's instructions.

Saffron Chicken in a Brick

Presoak a clay pot in water following the manufacturer's instructions. (Alternatively, use an ovenproof oval casserole into which the chicken will fit tightly.)

Using a mortar and pestle, grind the salt with the saffron, if using, to a fine powder. Add the cayenne. Season the chicken inside and out with this mixture and put the bunch of thyme inside the body cavity. Cut a slice off the top of each garlic head, exposing the white interiors. Replace the tops. Set the chicken, untrussed, breast up, in the clay pot. Trickle the olive oil over the breast. Put the garlic heads at each corner of the pot.

Cover and cook in a preheated oven at 450°F for 1¼–1½ hours until done. To check, prick the thickest part of the thigh with a skewer—the juices should run golden, not pink. Alternatively, jiggle the leg joints—they should move freely.

Serve the chicken and garlic on a large serving platter. Each person should squeeze the creamy garlic purée out of the heads and eat with the meat.

Note: Many manufacturers recommend that their ceramic containers be put into a cold oven. Allow extra time for the oven to heat up, about 20–30 minutes.

¼ teaspoon powdered saffron or 4 pinches of saffron threads

1 teaspoon kosher salt or sea salt flakes

½ teaspoon cayenne pepper

3 lb. chicken, preferably free-range or organic

a bunch of fresh thyme

4 whole heads of garlic

1 teaspoon extra virgin olive oil

SERVES 4

Chicken Kiev

A Ukrainian contribution to Russian cuisine dating back to about 1900, Chicken Kiev is now a restaurant favorite all over the world. Butter alone was the original filling: today, garlic and parsley flavor the butter and there are many other alternatives, some more successful (and appropriate) than others. Strictly the correct cut is the suprême of chicken—a boned breast with the first wing joint still attached—but few butchers or poulterers still prepare it in this way.

It can be easier to buy the same cut, but without the wing joint "peg" bone: please yourself. The preparation processes are not difficult, but they need exactness in timing and in temperature: do allow enough time. The results are worth the effort: it tastes absolutely delicious. The packages are cut open at the table—cut them carefully, or the hot butter could spurt everywhere.

Chicken
Kiev

6–8 garlic cloves, crushed

1½ cups chopped fresh parsley

6 tablespoons butter, at room temperature

½ teaspoon salt

freshly ground black pepper

4 suprêmes of chicken, about 8 oz. each
or 7 oz. boneless*

⅓ cup all-purpose flour

4 eggs, lightly beaten

2⅔ cups dry breadcrumbs

pure olive oil, for frying,

about 2 quarts

SERVES 4

*Suprêmes are skinless breast portions, preferably with
the first wing bone or "peg" bone left intact.

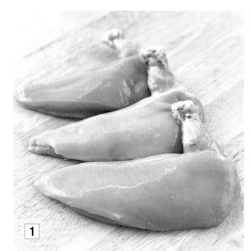

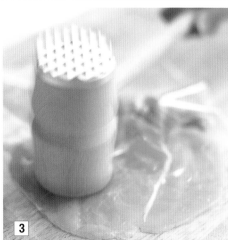

1 Prepare the suprêmes, preferably including the traditional wing or "peg" bone.

2 To make the stuffing, put the garlic and parsley in a food processor and pulse until finely chopped. Put in a bowl and stir in the butter, salt, and pepper. Transfer to a piece of wax paper and, using a spatula, spread the mixture into a rectangle 3 x 2 x ½ inch thick. Using a sharp knife, mark into 3-inch "fingers." Freeze for exactly 20 minutes to harden.

3 Put a suprême between 2 sheets of thick plastic or wax paper—the curved "peg" bone should be upwards and visible, and the skinned surface downwards. Using the flat side of a meat mallet or rolling pin, beat out and flatten the chicken, avoiding the bone area, but getting the outer edges wafer thin so they will seal easily. Do not make any holes. The chicken should roughly double in area. Prepare the other suprêmes in the same way. If the small fillet (tender) breaks off, beat and flatten it out separately.

4 Remove the parsley butter from the freezer and set each "finger" lengthwise about 1 inch below the wing joint. Fold up the base flap (the short side opposite the wing) to enclose part of the butter. Press to seal. Fold the left flap firmly over, then roll up each package to the right, completely enclosing the butter and making a neat, rolled cylinder. The wing bone, if any, should be at the top. Put on a nonstick surface such as thick plastic or wax paper. Prepare the other packages in the same way.

5 Dip each parcel in flour, pat off any excess flour, then dip each parcel in the beaten egg.

6 Working on one at a time, lift carefully into the crumbs and pat them well in all over. Put the completed, crumbed packages on wax paper and chill, uncovered, for 1 hour. Remove the chilled, firm packages. Repeat the egg and crumb coating process. Return to the refrigerator to chill for a further 2 hours.

7 Heat the oil in a deep-fryer or deep, heavy saucepan with a frying basket, to 360°F or until a small cube of bread will brown in 35–40 seconds. Using tongs, lower the packages, 1–2 at a time, into the hot oil. They must be well covered by oil and not touching. Cook the packages for 4½–5 minutes, then turn over carefully, using tongs and a spatula. Cook a further 4½–5 minutes.

8 Drain on crumpled paper towels, then serve whole on heated dinner plates.

Note: If the parcels brown too quickly, remove them from the oil with tongs and finish cooking in a preheated oven at 350°F for a further 10–15 minutes. They must be completely cooked through, but there is no way of checking except by cutting through and thus spoiling the whole effect.

Chicken with Forty Garlic Cloves

This classic French pot roast is ancient in provenance and produces a succulent, sweet bird. The mellow, fruity-flavored garlic cloves are eaten with the chicken and its juices—you can also mash them onto slices of baguette. Traditionally a "luting paste" or dough of flour and water was used as a seal between the dish and its lid. These days a good heavy oval cocotte or cast-iron enameled casserole such as Le Creuset is a much better bet, but if in doubt use the old system.

⅔ cup all-purpose flour

40 garlic cloves, peeled

1 teaspoon kosher salt or sea salt and freshly ground black pepper

¼ cup red wine

3 lb. roasting chicken

1 large sprig of fresh bay leaves

4 tablespoons butter or olive oil

1 baguette, to serve (optional)

SERVES 4

To make a seal of luting paste, put the flour in a bowl, add 3–4 tablespoons water and mix to a dough. Knead into a long sausage shape, 1 inch longer than the circumference of your casserole dish. Cover with plastic wrap or a damp cloth until ready to use.

Put the separated, peeled garlic cloves into a heavy, oval, flameproof casserole, barely bigger than the bird itself so it makes a snug fit. Add half the butter or oil and half the salt and pepper. Pour in all the wine.

Rub the bird with the remaining butter or oil and sprinkle with the remaining salt and pepper. Push the sprig of bay leaves inside the cavity. Press the sausage of dough, if using, around the rim of the casserole. Bring to a boil over a high heat for 10–15 minutes (if using a cast-iron casserole), then ram the lid on top to make a seal. Transfer to a preheated oven and cook at 375°F for 1½ hours, undisturbed. (If using a ceramic casserole, put in a cold oven, turn to the highest temperature and heat for 50 minutes, then reduce the heat to 375°F and continue cooking for 1½ hours.)

Break the pastry seal and uncover the casserole. Bake for a further 10–20 minutes at the same temperature until golden and aromatic. Carve and serve with slices of baguette—the garlic purée is spread over the baguette and served alongside the chicken.

Note: If you like, to be authentically French, before cooking, locate the wishbone of the bird and use your fingers and a small sharp knife to wiggle it free. Remove it without cutting the skin. This is usual for many traditional cooks: it makes carving easier.

Africa and the Middle East

From the fascination of sweetened chicken in fine pastry layers in Marrakesh to the exotically sumac-spiced chicken in flatbreads in Syria, chicken has long enjoyed a significant role in the cuisines of Africa and the Middle East. A pullet in a Tunisian medina, the strutting Nigerian cockerel, the squawking fowl behind a halal butcher's shop in Beirut, or a hen scratching happily in a South African garden: all these brave birds will result in some delicious dish. Because chicken is too expensive in many of these countries to be an everyday ingredient, it is all the more prized.

Chicken Kabobs

1 lb. boneless chicken breasts and thighs, cut into 1-inch cubes

¼ cup extra virgin olive oil

1 teaspoon dried oregano

½ teaspoon sea salt

1 teaspoon cracked black pepper

freshly squeezed juice of 1 lemon

TO SERVE

8 inch cucumber, half sliced, half grated coarsely

½ cup plain yogurt

2 garlic cloves, chopped

¼ cup chopped fresh mint or flat-leaf parsley, plus extra sprigs

½–1 teaspoon salt, to taste

4 flatbreads such as lavash, village bread, or halved pita bread

1–2 tomatoes, diced

¼ head crisp lettuce, such as romaine, chopped

1 red onion, sliced into rings

4 metal kabob skewers, oiled

SERVES 4

In many Arab countries, the kabob is king. Usually made of ground lamb or beef, they are pressed onto broad metal skewers and suspended over long troughs of glowing coals. But there is a chicken alternative, usually marinated in aromatic spices and herbs. The char-grilled result is wrapped in the local flatbread—lavash, khoubiz, pita, or naan—together with cucumber, yogurt, and other favorite Middle Eastern accompaniments. Wraps are popular all over the world, but nowhere more so than here.

Push the chicken onto the skewers and set in a shallow glass or china dish. Mix the oil, oregano, salt, pepper, and lemon juice in a pitcher, then pour the mixture over the chicken. Marinate for 10 minutes. Preheat an outdoor grill or broiler and cook the kabobs for about 5–8 minutes on each side or until the chicken is firm and white right through.

Put the grated cucumber in a strainer and squeeze it dry. Put in a bowl and mix with the yogurt, garlic, mint or parsley, and salt. Gently warm the bread and, if using pita bread, cut in half and open out the pocket.

Pull the cooked chicken off the skewers and divide between the breads, add the sliced cucumber, tomatoes, lettuce, and onion, spoon in some yogurt mixture and herb sprigs, wrap or roll up in wax paper, then serve.

Many Moroccan dishes are seasoned with subtle, ready-mixed spice combinations, mixed to order in the souk or bazaar. This chicken dish uses only four: two of which are used to rub into the skin of the chicken. If you can't find real saffron powder, double the amount of paprika and use half of that to help color the chicken. The apricots grow plump and juicy with blanching and give the chicken dish a good balance of sweet, salty, and sour flavors.

Chicken Tagine with Apricots

½ teaspoon ground turmeric

½–1 teaspoon saffron powder

3 lb. chicken, cut into 8 or 10 pieces

8 oz. dried apricots, about 1 cup

3 tablespoons butter or olive oil

2 onions, chopped

½ teaspoon ground ginger

½ teaspoon paprika

½ teaspoon crushed black peppercorns

1 teaspoon salt

a handful of fresh parsley, tied with twine

1 crisp apple such as Granny Smith, cored but not peeled, then cut into 8 pieces

mint sprigs, to serve (optional)

SERVES 4

Mix the turmeric with the saffron, then rub it all over the chicken pieces. Put the apricots in a small saucepan, add 1 cup boiling water, bring very gently to a boil, cover with a lid, then simmer for about 10 minutes.

Heat the butter or oil in a large flameproof casserole, add the onions, and sauté for 5 minutes, stirring. Add the ginger, paprika, peppercorns, and salt. Put the chicken on top.

Add 1½ cups cold water to the apricots, then pour the apricots and their liquid over and around the chicken.

Add the parsley, bring to a boil, cover with a lid, then reduce to a simmer, and cook, undisturbed, for 20 minutes. Add the apple. Simmer for a further 10–15 minutes, adding a little extra water if it looks too dry (the fruit absorbs much of the water).

Remove and discard the parsley. Serve the tagine with couscous or plain rice, topped with a few mint sprigs, if using.

Chicken Piri-Piri

Piri-Piri, in Portugal, refers to the tiny, searingly hot chiles that are a local passion. Fresh or dried, these are put into vinegar and left to infuse, giving a fiery sauce, *molho piri-piri*. It is an idea that turns up all over the world; in South Africa, Brazil, Cuba, and India. This version of the classic Piri-Piri has both Portuguese and South African influences.

To prepare the game hens or squab chickens, cut them in half down the breast and back using poultry shears and cut out and discard the backbone. Beat each half out flat with a cleaver or meat mallet. Pat dry with paper towels. Set on an oven tray with the potato and orange wedges tucked in and around them. Slash the skin twice on the outer curve of each leg (thigh and drumstick). Put the garlic, orange cubes, oil, and salt into a blender and purée for about 30 seconds. Pour the mixture over the chicken, orange, and potatoes.

Preheat the oven to 350°F, add the chicken, and bake, uncovered, for 20 minutes. Increase the heat to 400°F and continue cooking for a further 20–30 minutes or until the hens or squab chickens and potatoes are done. (Pierce the meat near the bone—it should be opaque right through, with no pink.)

Meanwhile, to make the Piri-Piri Dressing, put the vinegar, chiles (pierced with a toothpick if fresh), peppercorns, and wine into a screwtop shaker bottle with a plastic nozzle (just like you see in all the diners). Shake well to mix.

Remove the hens, potatoes, and orange wedges from the oven, transfer to a serving platter, and drizzle with the pan juices. Serve the Piri-Piri Dressing separately.

2 Cornish game hens or squab chickens

6 baking potatoes, cut into wedges

1 whole orange, unpeeled, half cut into wedges, half into ½-inch cubes

4 garlic cloves, crushed

⅓ cup extra virgin olive oil

1 teaspoon salt

green salad, to serve

PIRI-PIRI DRESSING

1 cup red wine vinegar

1–1½ oz. fresh hot red chiles or ½ oz. dried

1 teaspoon black peppercorns

½ cup port, Madeira, or dry sherry

SERVES 4

Moroccan B'stilla

North Africa is a wonderland of fascinating food tastes and styles. The classic version of *b'stilla* uses pigeon, but I use a cooked chicken, moist and juicy, with bones removed. This pie makes a grand gesture: save it for a celebration—it is gorgeous, superbly exotic, and delicious.

Sprinkle the salt all over the chicken: this will help balance out the sweet, scented tastes. Put 6 of the eggs and the extra egg white into a bowl and add the chicken stock and scallions. Whisk to mix. Put ¼ cup of the melted butter into a skillet, then stir in the scrambled egg mixture. Stir over medium heat until it is creamy and nearly set. Set aside to cool.

Mix the cinnamon and sugar in a small bowl. Grind the Spice Mix ingredients to a powder.

Unwrap the phyllo and unroll it. Cover with a damp cloth. Arrange 6–8 overlapping sheets of phyllo in the prepared pan so that much of it overlaps the edges and hangs down. Brush with melted butter (kept warm over boiling water). Sprinkle with some of the cinnamon-sugar mixture. Repeat this process twice more to make the basis of a strong, spicy crust.

Spoon a little more than half the egg mixture over the pastry. Repeat the phyllo-layering process using another 6–8 sheets overlapping, with each layer buttered, spiced and sugared. Add a close-fitting layer of chicken pieces, then sprinkle with the almonds, scallions, Spice Mix, and saffron, if using. Cover with the remaining egg mixture, then add the parsley. Add 6–8 more sheets of pastry, and brush with butter, and sprinkle with the cinnamon, and sugar. Push the pastry down firmly and tuck in the edges between the filling and the side pastry sheets (rather like making a bed!). Fold the overhanging pastry into the center and pat firmly into place. Scrunch up any remaining unbuttered pastry into a rosette shape and set it in the center.

Brush the top of the pie (not the rosette) with the remaining egg yolk and sprinkle with any remaining cinnamon-sugar mixture. Bake in a preheated oven at 350°F for 40 minutes. Increase the heat to 400°F and bake for a further 20 minutes or until crisp, golden, and aromatic. Remove from the oven and let cool in the pan for 10 minutes. Remove from the pan, then serve in big wedges, dusted with confectioners' sugar.

1 tablespoon salt

3 lb. freshly cooked chicken, without skin or bone, and cut into 2-inch chunks

7 eggs, 1 separated

½ cup chicken stock

2 sticks salted butter, melted

¼ cup ground cinnamon

¼ cup superfine sugar

32–42 sheets phyllo pastry dough, about 1 ½ lb.

1 cup blanched almonds

8 scallions, chopped

½ teaspoon saffron powder (optional)

¼ cup chopped, fresh, flat-leaf parsley

2 tablespoons confectioners' sugar, to serve

SPICE MIX

½ teaspoon ground ginger

½ teaspoon ground cinnamon

½ teaspoon cardamom pods

½ teaspoon cumin seeds

½ teaspoon ground turmeric

½ teaspoon black peppercorns

a roasting pan or large, 10-inch, loose-bottom cake pan

SERVES 8–10

Jollof Rice

This is a famous, much-adapted, one-pan chicken-and-rice dish originating in the kingdom of Jollof in West Africa. This dish is now a favorite wherever African-American and Caribbean communities thrive, as well as in its original home. The ham, peas, and canned tomatoes are clearly modern additions, but none the worse for all that. The cinnamon is optional, but delicate.

Heat the peanut oil in a large, heavy saucepan. Toss the chicken in the paprika to coat. Sauté in 2 batches over a medium heat for about 5 minutes. Add the onions, garlic, chiles, cinnamon, allspice, turmeric, and rice. Add the tomatoes and their juice, the chicken stock, and carrots.

Bring to a boil, then reduce to a simmer. Cover with a lid and cook, undisturbed, for a further 20 minutes.

Add the ham and peas and stir. Cover again and simmer for a further 8–10 minutes or until the rice is fluffy, the liquid almost all absorbed, and the peas and ham heated through.

Serve with wilted greens such as collard greens or cabbage, or more authentically with dasheen, gboma, or callaloo, also known as elephant ears.

Note: Either remove and discard the chiles before serving or warn guests they are there.

¼ cup peanut oil

8 chicken pieces, such as thighs, drumsticks, or breasts, or a combination

2 tablespoons hot paprika

2 onions, sliced

4 garlic cloves, chopped

2 hot bird's eye or other hot chiles, slit twice lengthwise

1 cinnamon stick, halved (optional)

½ teaspoon ground allspice

1 teaspoon ground turmeric

1 cup long grain white rice

2 cups canned chopped tomatoes in juice

2 cups chicken stock

2 carrots, cut into 2-inch strips

8 oz. ham, cut into ½-inch cubes, about 1½ cups

2 cups fresh or frozen green peas

SERVES 4–6

Nigerian students I met at university made stunning peanut and chile-based stews. This version needs the flavorful, well-exercised birds found in halal markets or farm shops, inexpensive and scrawny. Not keen? You could substitute ten free-range drumsticks or thighs, each cut into two pieces. You'll need a cleaver for this—or an obliging butcher.

Nigerian Peanut and Chicken Stew

Put the onions, salt, ginger, lemongrass, and lemon or lime juice into a large, heavy saucepan. Cover with the chicken and sprinkle with the crushed chiles.

Cook on a high heat until it is steaming hard, then cover the pan and reduce to a low simmer. Cook for 40 minutes (older birds) or 20 minutes (tender cuts). Put the peanut butter, tomato purée, and chicken stock in a bowl, stir well, then stir into the pan.

Return to a boil and stir well. Cover, reduce the heat, and simmer gently for a further 15–20 minutes. Sprinkle with parsley and serve.

Typical accompaniments include large, soft dumplings, couscous, rice, or bread for mopping up the generous amount of very rich sauce.

2 onions, sliced

2 teaspoons sea salt flakes

2 inches fresh ginger, peeled and shredded

2 stalks fresh lemongrass, about 8 inches total, split lengthwise almost to the base

juice of 2 lemons or 4 limes, about ½ cup

3 lb. chicken (a boiling fowl if possible), cut into 20 pieces, or 20 drumsticks or thighs

½–1 tablespoon crushed dried red chiles

⅔ cup smooth peanut butter

3 tablespoons tomato purée

⅔ cup boiling chicken stock

a bunch of fresh parsley, chopped, to serve (optional)

SERVES 4

The **Indian Subcontinent**

India is the source of some of the world's great chicken dishes—not surprising, since the bird is native to this area. One of the oldest breeds in fact is called the Indian Runner (a bird with very long legs!). The Indian Subcontinent boasts most of the world's major religions—Hindu, Muslim, Syrian Christian and Catholic, Buddhist, Jain, and Sikh. Beef is forbidden to Hindus, and pork to both Hindus and Muslims, so—apart from the vegetarian Jains and the orthodox Hindus of South India—all the other religious groups accept chicken. It is therefore the star of many of the great Indian dishes.

Butter Chicken

No matter how virtuous and restrained my friends are about their low-calorie, low-fat diets, this is the dish for which all rules are broken. Upmarket Indian chefs despise this recipe—whether for its blandness or its simplicity I do not know—but it is outrageously popular as a restaurant dish and easily made at home. If there is an Indian market where you live, ghee and fresh curry leaves will be easy to find—otherwise use fresh bay leaves: either fits the bill perfectly.

20 fresh curry leaves or 6 fresh bay leaves

1 teaspoon coarse salt

6 tablespoons butter ghee or clarified butter

2½ lb. chicken breast quarters, skin removed and discarded

3 garlic cloves, crushed

½ cup plain yogurt

1 teaspoon freshly ground black pepper

SERVES 4

Finely slice 16 of the curry leaves or 2 of the bay leaves. Using a mortar and pestle, pound them together with the coarse salt. Mash in 2 tablespoons of the ghee or clarified butter, then rub the mixture all over the bird. Put in a roasting pan, then cook in a preheated oven at 350°F for about 50 minutes.

Set the chicken and the remaining whole leaves in a shallow ovenproof dish. Heat the remaining ghee or butter but do not let it brown. Beat it and the garlic into the yogurt and pour all over the chicken. Bake at the same temperature for 10–15 minutes or until hot and well done. The sauce may seem to separate a little, as it throws out the oil—do not worry, this is normal and a sign that the butter has reached its most delicious stage.

Serve sprinkled generously with black pepper. Dhaal (lentil stew) and naan breads or rice would be suitable accompaniments.

Note: Many of the leading chefs in India have abandoned the traditional practice of coloring their dishes with food dyes. The popular idea of butter chicken used to include a creamy orange sauce—this version is more modern.

step-by-step

Tandoori Chicken

The tandoor is a clay oven and its Indian version originates in the Punjab, as do many of the Indian restaurant dishes familiar in other parts of the world. This is interesting, since most of the Indian restaurant chefs outside India come, not from the Punjab, or even from India, but from Bangladesh, and many of those come from just one place in Bangladesh—the northern city of Sylhet.

Since tandoor ovens can be hard to come by in most people's houses, I have adapted the traditional method so the skewers can be cooked on an outdoor grill or under a broiler—or even in the oven.

This recipe is based on the one used in Chef Manjit Gill's Bokhara Restaurant in Delhi's Maurya Sheraton hotel. If you ever have the good fortune to visit Delhi, go there—it is among the world's best.

step-by-step

Tandoori Chicken

1½ lb. boneless, skinless chicken, cut into pieces, about 1 x 1½ inches

1 tablespoon butter ghee or clarified butter, for brushing

FIRST MARINADE

1 tablespoon salt

2 inches fresh ginger, peeled and grated

3 garlic cloves, crushed

2 tablespoons rice vinegar

SECOND MARINADE

5 tablespoons grated mild Monterey Jack or Cheddar cheese

1 small egg, beaten

3–4 green chiles, seeded and chopped

a large bunch of fresh cilantro, chopped

1 tablespoon cornstarch

½ cup light cream

TO SERVE

2 lemons, 1 squeezed, 1 cut into wedges

1 red onion, finely sliced into rings

salad leaves

8 metal skewers

SERVES 4

1 Put the ingredients for the first marinade in a glass or china bowl and mix well. Pat the chicken pieces dry with paper towels, add to the bowl, and stir well. Set aside for about 15–20 minutes.

2 To make the second marinade, put the cheese, egg, chopped chiles, cilantro, cornstarch, and half the cream into a blender or food processor and pulse to mix.

3 Drain the chicken from the first marinade and discard the liquid.

4 Put into a clean bowl and add the blended second marinade. Stir well, then massage the mixture into the chicken using your fingers. Stir in the remaining cream and marinate for about 30 minutes.

5 Thread 3–4 pieces of chicken onto each skewer. Cook for about 6–8 minutes on a preheated outdoor grill, under a hot broiler,

or in the oven at 400°F for 8–12 minutes until half-cooked (put a tray underneath to collect the drippings).

6 Remove the skewers from the heat and set them upright in a bowl for 2–3 minutes so excess moisture can drain away.

7 Baste with melted ghee or clarified butter and return to the grill or broiler until done, about 8–10 minutes, or a few minutes longer if cooking in the oven.

8 (Page 72) Brush with the juice of 1 lemon and serve with finely sliced onion, torn salad leaves, and lemon wedges.

Tamil Coconut Chile Chicken

The seafaring Portuguese introduced chiles to the beautiful Tamil Nadu region of South India and Tamil dishes make the most of them. Since many people are vegetarians, this chicken dish is unusual. Local birds are hardy, free-range specimens—I have substituted tender Western chicken and so the cooking time is relatively brief, but please yourself in this matter. Allow a much longer simmering time if you choose an older bird and suit the volume of fresh chile to your own palate: Tamils prefer it incendiary. To mellow some of the heat, remove the chile membranes as well as the seeds.

4–6 tablespoons butter ghee, clarified butter, or peanut oil

2 onions, sliced

4 garlic cloves, crushed

2 inches fresh ginger, peeled and grated

2–4 green chiles, seeded and chopped

8 skinless chicken pieces, patted dry with paper towels

1 cup boiling chicken stock or water

2 cups canned coconut milk

2 tablespoons freshly squeezed lime juice

2 tablespoons all-purpose flour

2 cups chopped fresh cilantro

salt

ROASTED SPICES

1 teaspoon crushed dried chiles, bruised

1 tablespoon coriander seeds, bruised

1 teaspoon black peppercorns, bruised

1 teaspoon cumin seeds or caraway seeds

1 tablespoon ground turmeric

SERVES 4

To roast the spices, put the dried chiles, coriander seeds, peppercorns, cumin or caraway seeds, and turmeric into a dry skillet and stir-fry them for 1–2 minutes until aromatic. Push the spices to one side, add half the ghee, clarified butter, or oil to the skillet, add the onions, and sauté for 4–5 minutes.

Add the remaining ghee or oil, garlic, ginger, half the green chiles, and the chicken. Stir-fry for about 8–10 minutes until the chicken is golden. Add the stock or water and about 1½ cups of the coconut milk. Bring to a boil, reduce to a simmer, and cook until tender, about 30–40 minutes. Stir in the lime juice, then add salt and extra green chile, to taste.

Mix the remaining coconut milk into the flour, then stir into the chicken mixture and increase the heat until the sauce thickens evenly.

Top with the chopped cilantro leaves and serve with other Indian dishes such as coconut rice or chapattis.

Cream, yogurt, nuts, and spices make this Moghul-influenced chicken dish from North India utterly delicious. Avoid the use of turmeric: this is a dish which cries out for proper saffron, both for beauty of color and for aroma and flavor. The finished dish is mellow: with a creamy softness. It is not a fiery hot dish—quite the opposite.

Chicken Korma

¼ teaspoon saffron powder or a large pinch of saffron threads, ground with a mortar and pestle

¼ cup milk

1½ lb. boneless, skinless chicken breast, cut into 2-inch cubes

6 tablespoons butter ghee or clarified butter

6–8 garlic cloves, crushed then chopped

2 onions, coarsely grated to a pulp

2 teaspoons garam masala

2 teaspoons Kashmiri chili powder or other mild red chili powder

⅔ cup heavy cream

½ cup plain yogurt

¼ cup ground almonds

¼ cup cashew nuts, half whole, half finely chopped

½–1 teaspoon salt

4 inches cucumber, skin on, finely sliced, to serve

SERVES 4–6

Mix the powdered saffron and milk in a large bowl. Add the chicken and toss well to coat.

Heat the ghee or butter in a large, heavy saucepan or casserole. Add the chicken and stir-fry for about 3–4 minutes at a moderate heat until seared on all sides.

Add the garlic and onions to the pan and stir-fry for a further 2–3 minutes. Add the garam masala and chili powder. Stir-fry for a further 2 minutes, or until the chicken is half-cooked.

Stir in the cream, yogurt, almonds, chopped cashews, and salt. Add about 3–4 tablespoons water, cover, and simmer gently for another 6–8 minutes, adding the whole cashews towards the end of this time. The sauce should be slightly reduced and it may have "split," but this is not a problem. Taste and adjust the seasoning, then serve with plain basmati rice and finely sliced cucumber.

Note: Garam masala can be bought in Indian food stores and specialty grocers. To make your own, put 2 tablespoons coriander seeds in a dry skillet. Add 2 tablespoons peppercorns, 1 tablespoon cumin seeds, the black seeds from 15 green cardamom pods, 10 whole cloves, 1 cinnamon stick, broken up, and 2 teaspoons freshly grated nutmeg. Transfer to a dry skillet and stir-fry until aromatic, about 5 minutes. Transfer to a mortar and pestle or clean coffee grinder and grind to a coarse powder. Cool. Use 2 teaspoons for this recipe and store the rest in a screw-top jar, preferably in the refrigerator.

Chicken Biryiani

An Indian or Pakistani biryiani is a layered dish of basmati rice and chicken or meat. It is intricately but mildly spiced, as is typical of Moghul cuisine. It is elegantly colored and flavored, usually with saffron, though in India turmeric is often used instead. It is a special occasion dish for a party. Delicious butter ghee, sold in cans in Indian stores, gives the authentic flavor, but you can use clarified butter.

3 lb. chicken, quartered

2½ cups chicken stock

1 green serrano (medium hot) chile, seeded and chopped

3 inches fresh ginger, peeled and sliced

2 cinnamon sticks, crushed

½ teaspoon sea salt flakes

2 onions

6 tablespoons butter ghee or clarified butter

1¼ cups basmati rice

20 green cardamom pods

6 whole cloves

¼ cup blanched almonds

¼ cup shelled pistachio nuts, blanched and skinned

½ cup dried mango pieces, raisins, or sultanas

1 teaspoon coriander seeds, crushed

1 teaspoon cumin seeds, crushed

4 garlic cloves, chopped

1 teaspoon saffron powder or 2 pinches saffron threads, crushed

a handful of fresh cilantro leaves, to serve

SERVES 4

Put the chicken pieces, stock, chile, ginger, cinnamon, and salt into a large, heavy saucepan or flameproof casserole. Bring to a boil, cover, reduce the heat, and simmer for 30 minutes or until fairly tender. Remove the chicken to a plate and set aside.

Pour off the liquid into a measuring cup and make up to 2½ cups with water if necessary.

Quarter the onions then separate into petal-like layers. Add the ghee or clarified butter to the saucepan and heat until melted. Add the onion petals and fry until golden. Remove with a slotted spoon and set aside on a small plate.

Add the rice, cardamom pods, and cloves to the pan and stir-fry for 2 minutes until the rice is browned slightly.

Return the chicken to the pan, then add the almonds, pistachios, dried fruit, coriander and cumin seeds, and garlic. Sprinkle with the saffron and cook for 2 minutes more.

Return the stock and the onions to the pan, bring to a boil, reduce to a simmer, cover, and cook, undisturbed, for a further 12–15 minutes. The rice should be tender and the liquid completely absorbed. Serve with fresh cilantro sprinkled on top.

Note: Though it is usual to remove the skin when cooking chicken in the Indian way, if you leave it on the flavor will be richer and even more delicious.

East and Southeast Asia

In the culinary paradise that is the East and Southeast Asia, chicken and pork are the major protein sources for the resolutely non-vegetarian population. (The non-meat-eating traditions of Buddhism are largely confined to the monkish lifestyle.) Chicken is usually cut up small and stir-fried, stewed, or threaded onto soaked wooden satay sticks and grilled over coals. It is always interestingly spiced and seasoned with some of the most complex flavors in the world. In Southeast Asia especially, the mildness of chicken is enhanced by the sweet-sour-salt balance, the flavors intriguingly fresh, with chile, lime, coconut, lemongrass, and fish sauce used as aromatics.

In Vietnam, this crisp, clean, sweet, salty salad would be made with cooked ground chicken. This one is made with poached chicken, but you could also use roasted instead. This is a wonderful lunch dish for a summer party.

Vietnamese Chicken and Peanut Salad

3 boneless chicken breasts, about 1½ lb.

1 teaspoon salt

¼ cup peanut oil

¼ cup finely sliced shallots or baby onions

¼ cup peanuts

sprigs of mint

about 25 ready-to-eat shrimp crackers (optional)

PICKLED VEGETABLES

1¼ cups white rice vinegar

1¼ cups sugar

1 tablespoon salt

a large wedge of white cabbage, about 8 oz., shredded finely

1 small cucumber, halved lengthwise, then sliced crosswise

1 carrot, finely sliced

2 celery stalks, finely sliced

1 lime, halved lengthwise, finely sliced crosswise

DRESSING

2 tablespoons peanut oil

2 tablespoons fish sauce, such as Vietnamese *nuóc mam*

1–2 red chiles, finely sliced

SERVES 4–6

Put the chicken in a saucepan and half-cover it with cold water. Add the salt. Bring almost to a boil, reduce the heat, cover, and simmer for 15 minutes. Remove the lid and turn the breasts over. Cover and cook for a further 5 minutes, then turn off the heat. Let stand for 10 minutes, then drain and shred into small pieces. Set aside.

Heat the oil in a small saucepan. Add the sliced shallots or onions and sauté until deep golden brown. Remove with a slotted spoon and drain on paper towels. Add the peanuts to the oil and sauté until dark and crisp. Remove with a slotted spoon and drain on paper towels. Reserve the oil.

To prepare the pickle, put the rice vinegar, sugar, and salt into a large saucepan and bring to a boil. Let cool. Put the cabbage, cucumber, carrot, celery, and lime slices into a glass or china bowl, pour over the vinegar mixture, then cover with plastic or a lid.

Marinate for 2 hours, then drain, reserving ½ cup of the pickling liquid in a bowl. To make the dressing, stir the peanut oil, fish sauce, and chiles into the bowl.

Divide the vegetables between 4 small bowls, add the chicken, and pour over the dressing. Sprinkle with the peanuts, shallots, and mint, then serve with the shrimp crackers, if using.

This must be one of the world's best-loved soups—utterly superb. Fresh lemongrass, galangal (like fresh ginger but crisper, more medicinal), kaffir lime leaves, and fiery bird's eye chiles will require a visit to an Asian store or supermarket. Powdered substitutes will not do. Buy extra of these fresh ingredients and freeze for later.

Spicy Thai Chicken Soup

Put the stock in a large saucepan and bring to a boil. Add the chicken, garlic, lemongrass, fish sauce, ginger, galangal, if using, scallions, and coconut cream.

Return to a boil, partially cover, reduce the heat to a high simmer, and cook for 5 minutes. Add the kaffir lime leaves, if using, the chiles, half the cilantro, and the shrimp.

Simmer gently for 5 minutes or until the chicken is cooked through and the shrimp flesh is densely white—do not overcook or the shrimp will be tough. Add the lime juice and serve in heated soup bowls, topped with the remaining cilantro leaves.

Note: Remove the chiles before drinking the soup: they are fiery, but leaving them whole and merely crushing them releases a gentle, not violent heat.

5 cups boiling chicken stock, preferably homemade

12 oz. boneless, skinless chicken breasts, finely sliced

2 garlic cloves, chopped

2 stalks fresh lemongrass, halved lengthwise

3 tablespoons Thai fish sauce (*nam pla*) or light soy sauce

1 inch fresh ginger, peeled and grated

1 inch fresh galangal, peeled and sliced (optional)

8 small scallions, quartered

⅓ cup coconut cream

4 fresh kaffir lime leaves, crushed (optional)

2 green bird's eye chiles, crushed

a large handful of fresh cilantro leaves, torn

8 oz. raw tiger shrimp, peeled or unpeeled*

freshly squeezed juice of 2 limes

SERVES 4: MAKES 6 CUPS

*Do not use cooked shrimp: the texture will be disappointing.

Chopstick Chicken Wontons

Many versions of wontons and wonton soup are found all over China. Making and shaping the wontons takes less time than you'd think—the main thing is to ensure a tight, effective seal. I buy wonton wrappers in bulk, wrap them in packs of 40, and freeze for future use: they defrost quickly and well. You can then make wontons at the drop of a hat—on a whim.

2 quarts boiling chicken stock, preferably homemade

4 scallions, sliced into long strips

1 package wonton wrappers, about 36*

WONTON FILLING

12 oz. uncooked chicken breast, minced

2 inches fresh ginger, peeled and shredded

2 red chiles, seeded and chopped

1 egg

2 tablespoons sesame oil, preferably unrefined

2 teaspoons sea salt flakes

1 teaspoon freshly ground black pepper

TO SERVE

¼ cup toasted sesame seeds (optional)

dipping sauces such as soy, chile, or yellow bean sauce

SERVES 4: MAKES 36

*Packages vary, but contain about 40 large (4-inch) or 70 small (3-inch) wrappers. Leftovers can be frozen.

Put the stock and scallions in a large, wide saucepan and bring to a boil. Reduce to a simmer and cover with a lid.

To make the wonton filling, put the ground chicken, ginger, red chiles, egg, sesame oil, salt, and ground black pepper in a bowl and mix well. Put 1 heaped teaspoon of the mixture in the center of each wonton wrapper. Dampen the edges with water and pinch them together tightly to form a triangle. Wet 2 of the folded points and pinch them together to seal, making them into a circle. Continue until all the filling has been used and freeze any leftover wrappers. Don't let the wontons touch each other or they may stick together.

Return the stock to a rolling boil and add the wontons to the pan all at once. Cook for 4 minutes, then, when they have risen to the surface, remove with a slotted spoon. Serve in little china bowls, sprinkled with sesame seeds, if using, and with some of the dipping sauce spooned over. Serve extra dipping sauce separately. Eat with chopsticks.

Variation
Alternatively, serve as a soup and sprinkle with vinegar (unorthodox but good). Wontons can also be served as a snack, followed by a clear soup.

step-by-step

Steamed Dumpling
Purses

The Cantonese name for these dumplings, *sui mai*, means "cook and sell." People buy them—freshly cooked and hot, direct from the steamers—from street hawkers or market stalls, then eat them plain or with a splash of hot, spicy, or salty sauce. Wherever there are Chinese communities, you will find these dumplings served in dim sum restaurants and tea houses.

step-by-step

Steamed Dumpling Purses

1 egg white, lightly beaten

2 teaspoons yellow bean paste

2 inches fresh ginger, peeled and finely grated

2 tablespoons light soy sauce

a large handful of fresh parsley, cilantro, or chives, finely chopped

4 scallions, finely sliced

8 canned water chestnuts, drained, rinsed, and finely chopped

1 lb. lean ground chicken

4 slices bacon, chopped, or 2 oz. ground pork

1 teaspoon ground white pepper

2 tablespoons vodka or Shaohsing (Chinese rice wine)

1¼ packets wonton wrappers, about 48*

cornstarch, for dusting

¼ cup chopped fresh parsley, cilantro, or chives, sliced scallions or green or red chile, for topping

soy sauce, sweet chile sauce, or lemon and garlic sauce, for dipping

SERVES 4–6: MAKES 48

*Packages vary, but contain about 40 large (4-inch) or 70 small (3-inch) wrappers. Leftovers can be frozen.

1 Put the egg white, bean paste, ginger, soy sauce, parsley, cilantro, or chives, scallions, and water chestnuts in a bowl and mix well.

2 Put the ground chicken, bacon or pork, pepper, and vodka or Chinese rice wine into a second bowl, mix well and set aside for 30 minutes. Beat the 2 mixtures together—use 2 spoons or clean, dry hands.

3 Using kitchen shears, trim the wonton wrappers into rounds, discarding the corners.

4 Put 1 wrapper in the palm of your hand. Add about 1 teaspoon of filling to the center. Cup up your fingers and palm to gather in the sides so they look like old-fashioned money purses.

5 Drop and tap each wonton gently onto a surface dusted with cornstarch: this flattens the bases so that they don't tip over while cooking. Add your choice of topping to each little purse. Continue until all are made.

6 Arrange the dumplings, not touching, on several layers of a large steamer, preferably bamboo. Cover with a lid. Cook, in batches if necessary, for 5–8 minutes until firm and the filling is opaque. (Top up the water in the base of the steamer frequently.) Serve accompanied by sauces or dips of your choice.

Indonesian Chicken Martabak

8 oz. cooked, boneless chicken (breast or thigh),
cut into ½-inch dice

1–2 teaspoons hot curry paste

2 tablespoons mango chutney

1 inch fresh ginger, peeled and grated

1 stalk fresh lemongrass, trimmed and
very finely sliced (optional)

about 8 large sprigs of fresh cilantro or mint leaves, sliced

1 package wonton wrappers*

1 egg white

peanut oil, for frying

DIPPING SAUCES

½ cup sweet chile sauce

½ cup Indonesian soy sauce (*ketjap manis*)
or regular soy sauce

SERVES 4: MAKES 20

*Packages vary, but contain about 40 large (4-inch) or 70 small
(3-inch) wrappers. Leftovers can be frozen.

This culturally hybrid, ravioli-type recipe contains ready-cooked chicken—poached, roasted, or rotisseried. Curry paste, Indian-style mango chutney, and Chinese wonton wrappers complete the picture. The filling, though unorthodox, is delicious.

Put the chicken into a food processor, add the curry paste, chutney, ginger, lemongrass, if using, and cilantro or mint. Process in brief bursts until coarsely chopped. Set aside.

Working with 8 wonton wrappers at a time, paint a border of unbeaten egg white around the edge of 4. Set 1 level teaspoon of filling in the center of each one. Cover with a second wonton wrapper and press down using the sides of your hands to seal the edges closed. Continue until all 20 are complete.

Pour 2–3 inches depth of oil into a heavy saucepan. Heat it until very hot, about 375°F, or until a small cube of bread browns in 30 seconds. Cook the wonton packages in batches of 4 for 6–8 seconds, pushing them down under the bubbling oil. Using tongs, turn them over and cook the second side for 6 seconds. As they cook, they expand, crinkle, blister, then turn deep gold. Alternatively, use a deep-fryer and cook in batches of 6–8. Drain on crumpled paper towels and keep them hot in the oven while you cook the remainder.

Serve 5 packages per person, with a choice of dipping sauces.

Just like Thai fish cakes (*tod man*), these little snacks will become a firm favorite. They make a perfect quick supper for three or snacks for six. Try them, with drinks, as pre-dinner snack foods accompanied by a dipping sauce, but make them smaller—this mixture will make about 40.

Tiny Thai Chicken Cakes

Using a meat grinder, food processor, or knife, finely chop the chicken to a coarse mixture.

Transfer to a bowl, then stir in the curry paste, kaffir lime leaves, garlic, ginger, cilantro, chiles, fish sauce, and half the cornstarch. Holding the beans in a bundle, shred them crosswise, wafer-thin, into "coins." Mix well into the chicken mixture. Divide in half, then in half again and so on until you have 32 portions. Press each into a flattened ball between your palms and dust with a little of the cornstarch.

Heat a large, nonstick skillet or stove-top grill pan until very hot. Add 1½ teaspoons of the oil and cook the chicken cakes, about 8–10 at a time, for 1 minute each side, pressing them down well with a spatula. Keep hot in the oven until the next 3 batches are cooked, adding an extra 1½ teaspoons of the oil to the skillet between each batch.

Serve hot with your choice of lime wedges, lettuce leaves, scallions, and steamed rice.

1 lb. boneless, skinless chicken breasts or thighs

2 tablespoons red or green Thai curry paste

8 fresh kaffir lime leaves, shredded hair-thin

4 garlic cloves, chopped

1 inch fresh ginger, unpeeled but grated

⅓ cup chopped fresh cilantro leaves

5–6 small red or green chiles, seeded and finely sliced

2 tablespoons Thai fish sauce *(nam pla)* or light soy sauce

¼ cup cornstarch

3 oz. green beans

2 tablespoons peanut oil, for frying

TO SERVE (OPTIONAL)

1 lime, cut into wedges

crisp lettuce leaves, such as iceberg or romaine

scallions, sliced lengthwise into curls

steamed rice

SERVES 3 OR 6

All around the world, noodle bars combining Japanese-style noodles, freshly made stock, barely cooked vegetables, and chunks of chicken or fish plus aromatics have become an everyday phenomenon. But the Japanese did it first, and best. The keynotes: beauty, simplicity, and clean, pure tastes.

1 lb. boneless, skinless chicken breasts or thighs, cut into ½-inch strips

5 cups boiling chicken stock

2 garlic cloves, chopped

2 inches fresh ginger, peeled and shredded

1 teaspoon Tabasco sauce

½ oz. dried Japanese seaweed, such as arame or wakame (optional)

1 tablespoon Japanese soy sauce

4 oz. dried Japanese udon noodles, or 8 oz. fresh

2 carrots, about 4 oz., very finely sliced

2 zucchini, about 4 oz., cut into julienne strips

2 tablespoons sesame seeds

1 cup bean sprouts

1 cup loosely packed baby spinach leaves

SERVES 4

Chicken with Udon Noodles

Put the chicken, stock, garlic, ginger, Tabasco sauce, seaweed, if using, and soy sauce into a large flameproof casserole. Bring to a boil, reduce the heat, then simmer for 8 minutes or until the chicken is tender. Taste and adjust the seasonings.

If using fresh udon noodles, rinse in cold water, then boil for 1 minute. If using dried noodles, boil for 6–8 minutes. Drain.

Meanwhile, bring a saucepan of lightly salted water to a boil, add the carrots, and simmer until nearly tender. Add the zucchini, return to a boil, and cook for another 1 minute. Drain, then add to the chicken broth, along with the cooked, drained noodles.

Put the sesame seeds in a dry skillet and sauté until toasted and golden.

Put a handful of bean sprouts into 4 large, heated soup bowls, then ladle the chicken, noodles, vegetables, and broth over the top. Scatter spinach leaves and sesame seeds on top. Serve hot, with soup spoons and chopsticks.

Yakitori Chicken

All over Tokyo, there are 24-hour snack bars, tiny restaurants, and food stands where chicken skewers are served in a sweet, glossy marinade. For "salarymen" and women, the long ride home seems more appealing after a fortifying snack of yakitori or a bowl of noodles. Yakitori is a quick, easy dish, but it can be marinated overnight in the refrigerator if you prefer.

½ cup Japanese soy sauce

¼ cup mirin (Japanese sweet rice wine), or white vermouth

¼ cup sake or dry sherry

2 tablespoons peanut oil

¼ cup sugar

1 inch fresh ginger, peeled and finely sliced

2 garlic cloves, chopped

1½ lb. boneless, skinless chicken pieces, 10 thighs or 4 breasts

16 scallions, quartered crosswise

2 tablespoons Japanese *shichimi togarashi*, *sansho* pepper, *furikake*, or toasted sesame seeds (optional)

16 bamboo satay sticks, soaked in water for 30 minutes

SERVES 4

To make the marinade, put the soy, mirin, sake or sherry, oil, sugar, ginger, and garlic into a blender and pulse to mix. Pour into a shallow glass or china dish. Cut the chicken into 1-inch square pieces, about ½ inch thick: there should be about 96. Add the pieces to the marinade. Stir well; marinate for at least 20 minutes or overnight in the refrigerator.

Preheat a broiler, stove-top grill pan, or outdoor grill. Thread 4 pieces of scallion and 6 pieces of marinated chicken onto each soaked skewer, pushing on the chicken so it sits flat and square, not packed tightly. Add the pieces of scallion crosswise, at intervals. Continue until all the skewers are prepared.

Cook the skewers 3 inches away from the heat source for 4–5 minutes each side. Pour the marinade into a small saucepan. Alternatively, pan-grill the skewers, 8 at a time, for about 1½–2 minutes each side, pressing them down well.

Bring the marinade to a boil, reduce the heat slightly, and boil down to about a third of its original volume: about 5 minutes. It should look thick and sticky.

Serve 4 skewers per person, glazed with some of the reduced marinade. Sprinkle with *shichimi togarashi*, *sansho* pepper*, furikake*, or sesame seeds, if using, then serve.

Note: *Shichimi togarashi* (a mixture of seeds, aromatics and other peppery tastes), *sansho*, and *furikake* are specialist seasoning products found in Japanese stores and, increasingly these days, in natural-food markets.

Indonesian Chicken Satays

This typical Indonesian dish has become extremely popular all over the world and this is great food for casual entertaining, as it can be prepared ahead and cooked at the last minute. Cook on an outdoor grill, under a broiler, or in the oven. The usual accompaniment is a peanut sauce, but lemon or lime squeezed over, some fresh cilantro, a dipping sauce, or even a spicy salsa are also good.

Put the brown sugar, lime juice, salt, pepper, garlic, soy sauce, coconut milk, molasses, and cilantro into a saucepan and bring to a boil. Simmer for 3–4 minutes, then remove from the heat and cool quickly over ice. Transfer to a shallow glass or china dish.

Slice the chicken lengthwise into even strips or ribbons. Add to the marinade and stir well to cover. Marinate for 20 minutes or up to 8 hours in the refrigerator. When ready to cook, preheat the outdoor grill or broiler (or the oven to 400°F). Drain the chicken, then push an even number of strips onto each satay stick, threading them on in pleated waves.

Brush each satay with a little of the peanut oil. Cook until firm and white right through, basting with the marinade towards the end of the cooking time.

Note:
• If using an outdoor grill, the skewers should be 2–3 inches above the coals and cooked for 2–3 minutes on each side.
• If using a broiler, cook 2–3 inches from the heat for 4–5 minutes on each side.
• If baking, cook in a preheated oven at 425°F for 15–20 minutes, turning over after 10 minutes.
• If cooking on a stove-top grill pan, preheat the pan, brush with oil, add the chicken, and cook for 2 minutes on each side, pressing down well with a spatula.

1 tablespoon brown sugar

freshly squeezed juice of 2 limes

½ teaspoon salt

½ teaspoon freshly cracked black pepper

3 garlic cloves, crushed

2 tablespoons soy sauce

⅓ cup thick coconut milk, from the top of the can

1 tablespoon molasses

a handful of fresh cilantro roots and leaves, chopped

4 skinless, boneless chicken breasts, about 1½ lb.

2 tablespoons peanut oil

16 bamboo satay sticks, soaked in water for 30 minutes

SERVES 4–6

Japanese Salt-Grilled Chicken

4 boneless, skinless chicken breasts
3 tablespoons sake or dry sherry
sea salt flakes

TO SERVE
4 scallions
Japanese pink pickled ginger

12 bamboo satay sticks, soaked in water for 30 minutes

SERVES 4

In this easy, minimal, but classic Japanese dish, sake is used to add sweetness and flavor and act as a tenderizer. Salt adds balance to the taste. These breasts are often skewered with three bamboo satay sticks in the shape of a fan: it stabilizes them for even cooking, but also looks elegant. Do not overcook this chicken: 12 minutes at the most.

Put each breast between 2 sheets of foil. Using your hand, a meat mallet, or a rolling pin, pound and flatten them to about half the original thickness. Transfer to a shallow glass or china dish. Pour over the sake, turn the chicken to coat, and set aside for about 5–10 minutes to tenderize.

Meanwhile preheat an outdoor grill or broiler. Remove the chicken from the dish and push 3 sticks into each breast to hold them flat.

Sprinkle a layer of salt over both sides of each piece of chicken. Put each piece on a sheet of foil and grill or broil, on the foil, for 4–5 minutes about 2–3 inches from the heat. Turn the chicken and cook for another 2–4 minutes. The chicken must be golden-brown, cooked right through, but not dry.

Serve with a scallion and a pile of pink pickled ginger. Eat hot, warm, or cold.

Almost all the world appreciates this dish, though few people stir-fry at the hot, fierce temperatures the Chinese do. Stir-fried also means "steam-stirred" in my book since the tender vegetables mostly cook in the aromatic steam. Use a sweet chile sauce, not a fiery Thai version or Indonesian sambal: this is a dish from China, after all.

Stir-Fried Chicken with Greens

2 tablespoons peanut oil

3 large skinless, boneless chicken breasts cut in 2-inch strips or cubes, about 1 lb.

2 inches fresh ginger, shredded

2 garlic cloves, sliced

8 oz. broccoli, broken into tiny florets, about 1 cup

8 scallions, halved crosswise

7 oz. green beans, halved and blanched in boiling salted water

1 red or yellow bell pepper, seeded and cut into strips

⅓ cup chicken stock or water

2 tablespoons sweet chile sauce

1 tablespoon light soy sauce

2 oz. snowpeas, trimmed and washed

2 oz. sugar snap peas, trimmed and washed

4 oz. baby bok choy leaves, trimmed and washed

noodles or rice, to serve

SERVES 4

Put the oil in a wok and heat until very hot but not smoking. Alternatively, use a large, preferably nonstick, skillet. Add the chicken and stir-fry over a high heat for 2 minutes, then add the ginger and garlic and stir-fry for a further 2 minutes.

Add the prepared broccoli, scallions, green beans, sliced bell pepper, and chicken stock or water. Cover and cook for a further 2–3 minutes. Stir in the chile sauce and soy sauce. Toss the still-wet snowpeas and sugar snap peas and bok choy leaves on top. Cover and cook for 1–2 minutes. Toss well and serve while tastes and colors are still vivid and textures crisp.

Hunan Chicken

Hunan is the centre of a distinctive, northern school of cooking with a number of crisp but flavorful dishes. This chicken dish is one of the most famous. First the pungent, spicy marinade flavors the chicken, then a light, crisp crust forms outside it and acts as a delicious contrast.

Pat the chicken thighs and drumsticks dry with paper towels. Prick each piece several times with a fork, to let the marinade penetrate well.

To make the marinade, put the toasted Szechuan peppercorns, sugar, ginger, scallions, and soy sauce into a food processor and work to a purée. Alternatively, use a mortar and pestle. Transfer the mixture to a plastic bag. Add the chicken pieces and turn to coat: massage in the marinade. Press out any excess air, seal tightly, and refrigerate for 1 hour.

To make the dipping sauce, put all the ingredients in a bowl and mix well. Transfer to 4 small dipping bowls. Set aside.

Put the cornstarch into a large shallow dish. Drain the chicken, then roll each piece in the cornstarch so it sticks on.

Pour 3 inches depth of oil into a heavy saucepan or deep-fryer and heat to 375°F, or until a cube of bread will brown in 30 seconds. Using tongs, add the chicken pieces in batches of 4–6. Deep-fry for 7–8 minutes on each side. Test: the flesh must be totally opaque and firm, right through to the bone. Remove and drain on crumpled paper towels, keeping the pieces warm in the oven while you cook the remaining chicken pieces.

Serve hot in 4 large bowls with chopsticks and the small bowls of dipping sauce, topped with green scallion shreds.

6 chicken thighs

6 chicken drumsticks

1 tablespoon Szechuan peppercorns, pan-toasted for 1 minute

1 tablespoon sugar

2 inches fresh ginger, peeled and grated

4 scallions, finely chopped

2 tablespoons soy sauce

⅓ cup cornstarch

peanut oil, for deep-frying

DIPPING SAUCE

¼ cup black bean sauce

2 tablespoons sweet chile sauce

½ cup tomato juice

2 tablespoons light soy sauce

2 scallions, finely shredded, and green ends reserved for serving

SERVES 4

Red-cooking—simmering in a strong soy-sauce mixture—is also applied to other foods, such as pork. Traditionally, the cooking liquid was kept and used again and again—known as a "master sauce." It is important to use a pan into which the bird fits snugly: this way it cooks evenly in a minimum of liquid. The dish can be served in different ways.

Red-Cooked Chicken

3 lb. roasting chicken

1⅓ cups cold jasmine tea or cold water

1⅓ cups dark soy sauce

⅔ cup Shaohsing (Chinese rice wine) or dry sherry

2 inches fresh ginger, unpeeled and finely sliced

4 whole star anise

2 cinnamon sticks

2 tablespoons sugar

1–2 teaspoons chile oil or sesame oil

SERVES 4–8

Rinse the bird inside and out. Pat dry with paper towels. Take a flameproof casserole into which the chicken will fit snugly. Add the tea or water, soy sauce, Shaohsing or sherry, ginger, star anise, cinnamon, and sugar and bring to a boil. Add the chicken (the liquid should half-cover the bird). Return to a boil, reduce the heat, cover, and simmer for 20 minutes.

Remove the lid and, using tongs, turn the chicken over in the pan. Cover and simmer for a further 20 minutes. Pour over the chile or sesame oil, baste the chicken for several minutes, then cover again, turn off the heat and leave, undisturbed, for 2 hours.

To serve, remove and drain the cooled chicken. Pour the cooking liquid, strained, into a sealable jar or airtight container. Reserve about a quarter and refrigerate the rest.

Cut the chicken into bite-sized pieces, arrange on a serving platter, and drizzle with the reserved cooking liquid. Serve with stir-fried greens, steamed rice, or cold noodles dressed with sesame oil. Alternatively, strip the chicken from the bones and pile it up on top of a salad of bean sprouts, shredded daikon, and cucumber, with a rice vinegar and oil dressing.

Note: The chicken may also be brushed with a glaze. Put 2 tablespoons arrowroot in a bowl and stir in ⅓ cup cold water. Heat 1½ cups of the hot cooking liquid, stir in the arrowroot mixture, and heat to a glossy, thick glaze. Pour over the bird and serve.

step-by-step

Bangkok Chicken

This classic green Thai curry is based on a recipe from the renowned Oriental Hotel in Bangkok. Curries like these are served with a selection of other dishes, such as steamed rice, plain bean thread noodles, and one or more vegetable dishes. Thai cooks would use incendiary amounts of chiles, often the tiny, blindingly hot, bird's eye chiles, but for Western palates I have reduced the quantity. Spice pastes—red, green, orange mussaman, and so on—are an intrinsic part of Thai cooking. This classic green spice paste makes double the amount you'll need, so you'll have extra to use in other dishes (freeze it if keeping for more than a few days). You can also buy ready-made paste in larger supermarkets and Southeast Asian or Chinese food markets, but homemade is always the best. Traditionally ground with a mortar and pestle, the food processor makes their preparation a work of seconds.

Bangkok Chicken

2 tablespoons peanut oil

4 skinless chicken breasts, about 1½ lb, quartered crosswise

⅔ cup chicken stock

2 cups canned coconut milk

4 oz. Thai "pea" eggplants or diced cucumber

1 teaspoon fish sauce or 1 teaspoon salt

freshly squeezed juice of 1 lime

a large bunch of fresh Thai holy basil or mint

boiled fragrant Thai rice, to serve

GREEN CURRY PASTE

5–6 medium hot green chiles, seeded and finely sliced

a small bunch of fresh cilantro, chopped

2 stalks fresh lemongrass, finely sliced

1 inch fresh ginger, peeled and finely sliced

1 inch fresh galangal, peeled and sliced (optional)

4 fresh kaffir lime leaves, shredded hair-thin, or 1 tablespoon shredded lime zest

2 teaspoons coriander seeds, crushed

1 teaspoon cumin seeds, crushed

4 scallions, chopped, or small red onions

4 garlic cloves, crushed

SERVES 4

1 Put all the Green Curry Paste ingredients in a food processor and grind to a smooth paste. Alternatively, use a mortar and pestle. Reserve half the mixture for this recipe and refrigerate or freeze the rest.

2 Heat the oil in a large, preferably nonstick, skillet or wok, add the chicken, and sauté for 2–3 minutes or until firm and golden. Turn the pieces over as they cook.

3 Add the reserved curry paste. Sauté, stirring, for 1 minute. Add the chicken stock and return to a boil.

4 Add half the coconut milk and the pea eggplants or diced cucumber and cook, covered, at a rapid simmer (not a boil) for 5 minutes. Using tongs, turn the chicken pieces over, then reduce the heat to a very gentle simmer. Add the remaining coconut milk and the fish sauce or salt and cook, uncovered, for a further 8–12 minutes.

5 Add the lime juice and sprinkle with Thai basil or mint. Serve with fragrant Thai rice.

1

Today the wine and food culture of these two countries are the envy of the world. Their talent for absorbing and integrating food styles from their immigrant communities means that superb European and Asian traditions have enriched the cooking, markets, and café scene. Asian, British, and Polynesian styles predominate in New Zealand, with Southeast Asian, Italian, Greek, and Middle Eastern influences in Australia. Chicken, a perfect vehicle for experimentation, is just as likely to be cooked in soy or fish sauce as in a tomato passata; or in coconut milk as often as wine.

Australia and New Zealand

Vietnamese Peppery Chicken

The Vietnamese community in Australia has made a huge contribution to local food culture. Char-grilling, using many different, spicy marinades, is one of their most popular cooking methods. These brochettes are pungent and spicy-hot—not for the faint-hearted. In a pinch, lemons could stand in for limes, but limes epitomize fresh Vietnamese flavors better.

1½ lb. boneless chicken breasts or thighs

2 tablespoons Szechuan peppercorns or green peppercorns

2 tablespoons black peppercorns

1 tablespoon sea salt flakes

¼ cup apricot preserves

4 garlic cloves, crushed

2 tablespoons fish sauce, such as Vietnamese *nuóc mam* or Thai *nam pla*

shredded zest and freshly squeezed juice of 2 limes

TO SERVE (OPTIONAL)

2 small romaine lettuces, leaves separated

2 small bundles bean thread noodles, soaked in hot water for 3 minutes

2 inches cucumber, sliced and diced

a handful of mint sprigs

12 bamboo satay sticks, soaked in water for 30 minutes
oiled foil, for baking

SERVES 4

Beat the chicken pieces flat using a meat mallet or the flat side of a Chinese cleaver: this will also tenderize it. Cut into 1-inch square pieces.

Dry-toast both types of pepper in a skillet, shaking constantly until aromatic but not scorched. Using an electric spice grinder, clean coffee grinder, or mortar and pestle, grind or pound until coarse and gritty. Transfer to a shallow glass or china dish, add the salt, preserves, garlic, fish sauce, and lime juice. Reserve some of the lime zest for serving and add the remainder to the dish. Mix to a sticky paste. Add the chicken pieces and stir until well coated. Push the chicken, 4 cubes at a time, onto the soaked satay sticks.

Preheat a broiler or outdoor grill. Set the chicken skewers about 3 inches from the heat and cook for 4–5 minutes on each side. Serve with a platter of the serving ingredients.

To eat, remove the chicken from the skewers, fill lettuce leaves with noodles and cucumber, add the chicken, then top with mint and the reserved lime zest.

step-by-step

Tea-Smoked Chicken

Asian-style tea-smoked foods have an ancient and undoubted allure. Fish is the usual food treated this way, but in Australia and New Zealand many other foods such as chicken and duck get this sort of treatment. The method used to be a way of preserving foods and it still is, but its main role is to enhance the flavor and texture while cooking. You will need a lidded wok for this recipe.

step-by-step
Tea-Smoked Chicken

4 boneless, skinless chicken breasts

GINGER MARINADE

2 tablespoons peanut oil

1 inch fresh ginger, peeled and grated

1 tablespoon vodka

2 teaspoons Chinese 5-spice powder

1 teaspoon sea salt flakes

1 tablespoon chile oil

SMOKING MIXTURE

¼ cup sugar

¼ cups flour

¼ cup green tea leaves

6 whole star anise

2 cinnamon sticks, crushed

SERVES 4–6

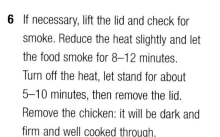

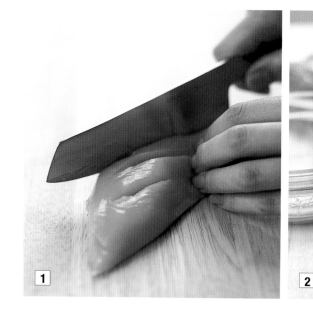

1 Pat the chicken dry with paper towels. Slash the skinned surface diagonally about 3–4 times.

2 Mix the marinade ingredients in a bowl, then rub all over the chicken, pressing into the cuts. Marinate for 30 minutes or overnight in the refrigerator.

3 Line a wok with foil, with the ends left hanging out. Put the smoking mixture ingredients in the wok and stir gently.

4 Set a metal rack in the wok, about 1–2 inches above the dry mixture. Arrange the chicken, evenly spaced, on the rack.

5 Put the lid on the wok and fold the foil ends over the lid. Put the wok on the stove at a high heat until you can smell smoke (though little or none should be escaping).

6 If necessary, lift the lid and check for smoke. Reduce the heat slightly and let the food smoke for 8–12 minutes. Turn off the heat, let stand for about 5–10 minutes, then remove the lid. Remove the chicken: it will be dark and firm and well cooked through.

7 Cut the chicken into diagonal chunks, fine slivers, or cubes, then serve. Eat as a snack, hot or cold, with dipping sauces of your choice (chile-soy or hoisin, red bean sauce diluted with stock and vodka, or even fish sauce, honey, and scallions). Alternatively, serve it over udon noodles, sticky rice, or even cellophane noodles, with a little chicken broth added.

Post-War immigration from Europe, especially Greece and Southern Italy, transformed Australia in many ways. The newcomers added their vivid, flavorful ingredients and marvelous food to the great local traditions of barbecues and the outdoor life. Even parks, sports grounds, and beaches feature public outdoor grills where whole families gather for long sunny picnics to enjoy food like this.

Sicilian Barbecued Chicken

Put the garlic, salt, butter, and Tabasco into a bowl and mash to a paste. Spread under and over the skin of the chicken. Set aside while you preheat an outdoor grill.

Set the rack about 4 inches from the heat, add the chicken, and cook for 20–30 minutes, depending on the cut. Turn the pieces with tongs from time to time, and move the tenderer cuts towards the cooler, outside areas of the grill as others continue to cook.

Meanwhile, to make the dressing, put the lemon and orange juices, the orange zest, olive oil, citrus liqueur, and barbecue sauce in a large, deep bowl. Beat well, then add the olives.

Add the hot, cooked chicken pieces to the bowl and turn them in the dressing. Serve the chicken, its dressing, and the olives with the parsley and lemon halves.

Variation
Instead of cooking on an outdoor grill, bake in a preheated oven at 400°F for about 1 hour or until done. Transfer to the bowl of dressing and proceed as in the main recipe.

4 garlic cloves, crushed and chopped

1 teaspoon kosher salt or sea salt flakes

2 tablespoons butter, at room temperature

½ teaspoon Tabasco sauce

4 lb. chicken, cut into 12 pieces

ORANGE DRESSING

freshly squeezed juice of 2 lemons

shredded zest and freshly squeezed juice of 2 oranges

½ cup extra virgin olive oil

2 tablespoons citrus liqueur, such as Grand Marnier, Cointreau, or Limoncello

2 tablespoons barbecue sauce

1 cup salt-cured black olives

TO SERVE

leaves from a few sprigs of flat-leaf parsley

2 lemons, halved

SERVES 4–6

Once upon a time, chicken wings were small, tough, and scrawny, barely worth a mention except for use in soups for their lovely gelatinous quality. Forget the past. Today, convenient packs of big, plump, meaty wings are an altogether different story. They are effortless, quick, inexpensive, and addictively enjoyable. They emerge from the oven sizzling, blistered, crunchy-crisp, and golden. Cook the wings with the tips up; in a furiously hot oven so that they caramelize—taking care not to burn your fingers in your eagerness.

Crisp-Baked Chicken Wings

16 large chicken wings, about 3½ lb.

½ teaspoon salt

½ teaspoon freshly ground black pepper

⅓ cup extra virgin olive oil

SERVES 4

Put all the ingredients in a large plastic bag. Inflate the bag, then twist closed and seal or hold it firmly. Shake the bag, bouncing its contents until the chicken wings are evenly coated with oil and seasonings.

Tip the wings out onto a shallow roasting pan or tray and arrange with all the wing tips pointing upwards. Cook towards the top of a preheated oven at 425°F for 35–45 minutes. They should be golden, crisp, and very hot.

Serve them just as they are and eat with your fingers. (Cold, they lose their stickiness and charm.) Lots of paper napkins and perhaps some finger bowls would be helpful.

Note: If the wings are small, 14 per pound or so, cook them the same way, but reduce the time by 10–15 minutes.

Variation
Add 2 tablespoons soy sauce to the bag, then steam the wings until tender, instead of baking them, about 20–30 minutes—they will be soft, not crunchy.

Spatchcocked Cornish Hens

"Despatch a cock!"—a command once shouted in British coaching inns in centuries past—meant that a customer had just ordered chicken. A spatchcocked bird is cut down either side of the backbone, which is then removed. The chicken is then thumped flat with the hand or a heavy cleaver. It cooks quickly and evenly—a very good method for cooking small birds such as Cornish hens.

2 Cornish hens

4 tablespoons salted butter

2 tablespoons Dijon mustard

4 garlic cloves, crushed

1 teaspoon freshly cracked black pepper

a handful of fresh basil or tarragon leaves, chopped, plus extra to serve

4 long metal or bamboo skewers, soaked in water for 30 minutes if bamboo

SERVES 2

If you are buying Cornish hens from a butcher, ask him to spatchcock them for you. To do this yourself, put the bird, breast down, on a board. Using poultry shears or kitchen shears, cut on either side of the backbone and remove it.

Open the bird out flat, then turn it over. Slide your fingers between the neck skin and breast muscles. Locate the wishbone, wiggle it free, then pull or cut it out without damaging the skin. Press down heavily to flatten the breast, wings, and legs. If you like, snap the wing joints and remove the wingtips: alternatively, tuck them underneath.

Using 2 skewers per bird, skewer them in and out from one side to the other through breast section and leg section, holding the bird flat. Pat the birds very dry with paper towels.

Mix the butter, mustard, garlic, pepper, and basil or tarragon to make a soft paste. Rub this over both sides of each bird. Set aside for at least 10 minutes or overnight in the fridge.

Preheat a broiler and set the birds on a foil-lined broiler pan, flesh side up. Cook about 4 inches from the heat until the skin is quite charred, about 15 minutes. Turn the birds over and cook for a further 15–20 minutes. Most of the cooking should be done with the bony surface uppermost, or the skin will overcook. If necessary, move the broiler pan closer to or further away from the heat.

Remove from the heat, take out the skewers, cut each bird in half down the breast, and serve sprinkled with more chopped basil or tarragon. Eat with your fingers.

Paprika Roasted Chicken

In New Zealand, when we were growing up, a roasted chicken was an occasional, rather special event—the era of intensively reared birds had yet to arrive. To me, still, a well-roasted chicken remains an easy but delicious treat. The recipe given here is my husband's favorite roasted chicken dish. It is cooked breast up and the skin becomes rosy, crisp, and almost like crackling when treated with dry seasonings in this way. Serve with a trickle of red wine sauce.

1 tablespoon hot paprika
1½ teaspoons salt
3 lb. chicken, free-range or organic
½ cup full-bodied red wine
1–2 tablespoons butter (optional)

a roasting pan with roasting rack

SERVES 4

Mix the paprika and salt in a small bowl or cup. Rub the mixture well into the skin of the bird and sprinkle some into the cavity. Set the chicken, breast upwards, on a rack set in shallow roasting pan, with the legs set wide apart, not trussed (not elegant, but it makes for quick and even cooking all over, especially around the thigh and lower breast areas).

Roast in a preheated oven at 425°F for 15 minutes, then reduce the heat to 375°F and roast for a further 1–1¼ hours or until juices from the thigh run clear yellow, not pink, when pierced. Transfer the chicken to a serving platter, return it to the turned-off oven and leave the door slightly open while you make the sauce.

Tip up the empty roasting pan and pour off all but 1–2 tablespoons of the fat (if there isn't enough, you will have to make up the quantity later with butter). Put the pan on top of the stove over a medium heat. Add the wine to the pan, stirring with a wooden spoon to dissolve all the residues.

Cook for 2–3 minutes or until the sauce bubbles and becomes syrupy. Add the butter at this stage if the sauce does not thicken—it will assist in the process.

Serve the chicken with the sauce. Suitable accompaniments include creamy mashed potatoes and a watercress salad.

Chicken Kataifi

Kataifi or kataif was brought to Melbourne, Australia, by Greek immigrants—Melbourne is said to be the second largest Greek city in the world. It is a fine, shredded-wheat pastry, traditionally used to make Greek sweetmeats. Recently I have seen it wrapped around shrimp before frying and once I tasted it as a crispy bed for chicken. It is fun to use. Go to a Greek or Middle Eastern food store to find the kataifi—it would take a lifetime to learn how to do it yourself. If none can be found, use crinkled-up phyllo pastry instead and treat in a similar way.

Shape the kataifi pastry into 8 little circular nests, hollowing out the center to take the filling. Set on a baking sheet. Brush generously with the melted butter and oil. Cook at the top of a preheated oven at 400°F for 10 minutes or until golden and crisp. Remove from the oven and pile up into 4 pairs of 2 nests.

Leave the oven at the same temperature. Mix the vinaigrette ingredients in a small bowl or pitcher, add the coriander seeds, honey, and garlic and stir until the honey dissolves. Put the chicken into an ovenproof dish and pour over the vinaigrette mixture. Transfer to the oven and cook for 15–20 minutes until the chicken is firm and white.

Pit the nectarines and plums and cut each fruit into 8 wedges. Add to the chicken, spooning over some of the marinade. Cook for a further 8–10 minutes until well heated through.

Spoon the hot chicken and fruit wedges into the warm kataifi pastry baskets, drizzle over the sauce, add sprigs of parsley, and serve hot.

8 oz. kataifi pastry or phyllo pastry

4 tablespoons butter, melted

2 tablespoons olive oil

2 teaspoons coriander seeds, crushed

¼ cup clear honey

2 garlic cloves, chopped

12 oz. chicken breast fillets or tenders (strips from underneath the breast)

2 large ripe nectarines

2 plums

small sprigs of flat-leaf parsley, to serve

VINAIGRETTE

¼ cup olive oil

1 tablespoon red wine vinegar

sea salt and freshly ground black pepper

a baking sheet, greased

SERVES 4

First know your chicken

FROM BIG TO LITTLE …

It is important to understand the difference between chickens. A commercially raised hen and a free-range roaster are not at all the same. There is a world of difference between a stewing chicken and an organic or free-range bird. They do not require the same cooking methods: they will taste different, be different sizes. Generally, you get what you pay for, but, whatever you choose, chicken is very versatile and responds well to numerous cooking techniques.

Whole roasting chickens

Whole roasting chickens are available fresh or frozen, in a range of sizes and qualities, from commercially raised to free-range and organic. Frozen birds should be thawed in the refrigerator. Check the body cavity for the giblets before cooking.

Sizes vary, but one can roast any size bird. At the supermarket look for:

Broiler-Fryers: 2–3½ lb.

Roasters: 4–6 lb.

Roasters generally have a higher fat content, making them suitable for roasting whole, or cooking on a rotisserie.

Stewing hens or boiling fowl

Mature hens about 10–18 months old and weigh 4½–6 lb. Though they are often commercially raised, they are still flavorful and economical. Halal and kosher butchers, ethnic markets, farmers' markets, and poulterers may still stock them. Because they are not as tender as a broiler or roaster, it is best to cook them slowly by a moist heat method such as stewing or use them to make soup.

Rock Cornish game hens

Miniature chickens, weighing up to 2½ lb., are 4–6 weeks old. Best broiled or roasted, one bird makes one serving.

Poussins or squab chickens

Immature birds, 4–6 weeks old, that weigh up to 1½ lb. Best for broiling, roasting, or grilling. They are very tender, but are not particularly flavorful so they need rapid browning and added flavor accents.

GRADES OF CHICKEN …

Commercially raised chickens

These are the most common chickens sold in supermarkets. They are cheap, tender, and popular, but lack flavor because they have been raised in a very short time, usually 51 days minimum, to keep costs down. They are suitable for most cooking methods, but the cook must add flavor by using herbs, spices, and fats such as olive oil or butter.

Free-range chickens

There are no government standards for free-range chickens, but free-range means that birds have access to the outdoors. Usually these birds are raised in portable houses that can be moved to new locations to allow them to forage for seeds, grasses, and other plants, insects, and worms. Some farmers believe this makes for a moister, tastier bird.

Kosher chickens

Checked by a rabbi to ensure that their vital organs are healthy, kosher chickens are believed to have the best flavor. As part of the process the birds are soaked in water to remove all traces of blood and then hand-salted. Some say these birds taste saltier than others do, even though they are rinsed after salting.

Organic chickens

Organically raised chickens are becoming more widely available and are not as expensive as they once were. They are produced by registered organic farmers and fed organically grown food with no additives, antibiotics, or organically modified products. They are labeled "certified organic" and in general are more flavorful, but thinner and more yellow than commercially raised birds.

The "crème de la crème"

The most prized chicken breeds and raising methods produce delicious birds. The most famous is the French *poulet de Bresse*, with superb texture and gamy flavor. They are older; they exercise and forage outdoors, and are hung before plucking to improve their flavor.

DRUMSTICKS, BREASTS AND BITS …

A wide range of cuts is available.

Breasts

BREASTS AND PARTIALLY BONED BREASTS

These portions have skin and at least some bone so they stay moist and keep their shape.

BONELESS CHICKEN BREASTS

Bones removed, but with skin intact.

BONELESS, SKINLESS BREASTS OR CUTLETS

White meat with no skin or bones. It can include the fillet or rib meat. Quick and easy to cook. Lean protein, versatile, but easily overcooked.

BREAST FILLETS OR TENDERS

The tiny finger-like projections from under each chicken breast, about ½ oz. each.

SUPRÊMES OR FRENCH BREASTS

Suprêmes are skinned breasts, still with part of the wing or "peg" bone still attached. In supermarkets, confusingly, the term can often mean boneless, skinless breast pieces but with no "peg" bone.

Wings

A complete wing consists of drumlet, winglet, and tip. They are sold in their entirety, with the winglet and drumlet separated, or with the tip removed. Wings are full of flavor and economical.

Legs

LEGS

Legs consist of thigh and drumstick. They are darker and richer than breast meat and can be boned and stuffed.

THIGHS

The top half of the leg with skin and bone, more flavorful than breast meat. It is also possible to buy them skinned and boned as "thigh fillets."

DRUMSTICKS

The lower half of the leg, including skin and bone. They are popular as finger food.

Other Cuts

QUARTERS

Sold as "breast quarters" including the wing and breast portion or "leg quarters" including the leg and lower breast portion. Sizes vary.

SCALLOPS OR PAILLARDES

Boneless, skinless chicken thighs or breasts, beaten out flat. They are sometimes sold in supermarkets, but are easy to make yourself.

GROUND CHICKEN

Chicken that has been skinned, boned, and then ground. Available in supermarkets or you can make your own using a meat grinder or a food processor.

Bits

GIBLETS

The neck, gizzard, heart and liver. They are sometimes found inside whole birds or sold separately at butcher shops.

CARCASS OR BACKS

The uncooked bones—excellent for stock, since some meat is still attached.

CHICKEN LIVERS

Available without the rest of the giblets.

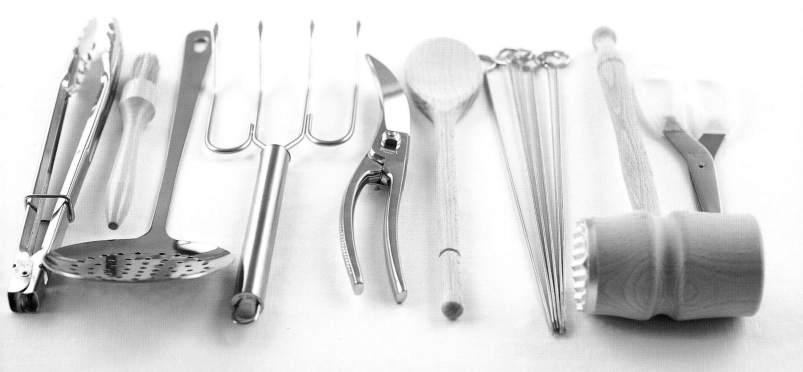

Cutting up

These days, most supermarkets sell trays of chicken pieces—all breasts, all thighs, all drumsticks, and so on. However, at any dinner party, you always find that there are people who like breasts, and people who like legs, and people who like both. So it's always good to be able to offer the choice. Most supermarkets sell whole chickens cut into pieces and butchers will also cut them up for you. Even so, it is useful to know how to do this task yourself.

1 Set the bird on its back. Push the legs outwards. Use a sharp knife to sever the flesh between the breast and leg sections and use a knife or poultry shears to sever the bone. Cut the legs through the knee joint, separating them into thighs and drumsticks (4 pieces).

2 Bend out and snap the wing joints. Cut off the wings with a knife, poultry shears, or shears (2 pieces). Snip off the wing tips.

3 Use poultry shears to cut up the middle of the breast section lengthwise.

4 Using a knife or poultry shears, cut up at an angle and separate the breast from the back section. Cut the back into 2 pieces. The breasts may also be cut in half crosswise giving 4 breast pieces.

5 There are now 10 (or 12) serving pieces: 2 thighs, 2 drumsticks, 2 back pieces (bony), and 2 (or 4) breast portions.

Note: Some people discard the backs or use them solely for soup. However, they contain the choice little "oysters" of tender flesh, also called *sots l'y laisse* (the bits other fools leave). I feel they are too good to waste.

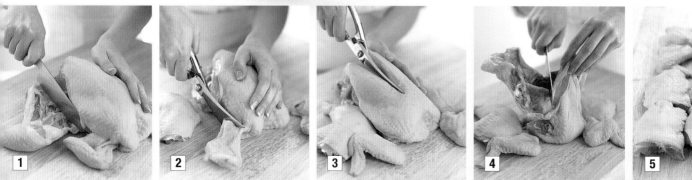

Stuffing

A good stuffing adds flavor, richness, and appeal to any chicken. Traditionally, in the days when a whole roasted chicken was relatively expensive and a special treat, stuffing a chicken meant it could feed more people.

There are a number of precautions that must be taken when cooking stuffed birds: filling the body cavity means that heat is not well conducted into the interior and this may result in an undercooked, even raw chicken—a definite health risk.

• Stuff the bird just before cooking.

• Remove the stuffing when cooked.

• It will take longer for a stuffed chicken to reach the proper temperature: Add about 35–50 minutes to the cooking time.

Breadcrumb stuffing

4 cups stale bread or breadcrumbs per 3 lb. bird
½ cup milk
1 stick butter, ½ cup olive oil, or 8 oz. bacon fat
2 onions, finely chopped
4 garlic cloves, crushed
8 slices bacon, chopped
½ cup chopped fresh herbs
2 tablespoons grated citrus zest (optional)
2 eggs, beaten
sea salt and freshly ground black pepper

Put the bread or breadcrumbs in a bowl and sprinkle with the milk. Let soak for 5 minutes, then squeeze dry, discarding the liquid. Return to the bowl.

Heat the butter, oil or bacon fat in a skillet, add the onion and garlic, and sauté until golden. Transfer to the bowl. Add the chopped bacon to the skillet and sauté until crisp. Transfer to the bowl. Add the chopped herbs and citrus zest, if using, then stir in the beaten egg. Cook about a spoonful of the mixture in a nonstick skillet, taste and season appropriately. Use to stuff the cavity and secure with a toothpick or skewer. Any leftovers may be folded in an envelope of foil and cooked beside the bird for the last hour of roasting time. Alternatively, cook separately at 350°F for 1 hour, then serve.

Refrigerate any leftovers: many prefer it served cold. Use within 24 hours.

Variations

• Substitute 2–3 oz. raw weight of other uncooked starch such as rice, couscous, oatmeal, or cracked wheat instead of the breadcrumbs.

• Suitable herbs include parsley, sage, thyme, tarragon, chives, marjoram, and celery leaves.

• Other flavorings may also be used, including black, white, or green peppercorns, harissa paste, chermoula, chopped fresh chiles, nutmeg, mace, allspice, or cinnamon.

OTHER STUFFINGS

You can also add breadcrumb or other stuffings to smaller cuts of chicken between skin and flesh, or make a pocket inside a boneless piece of chicken.

Butter stuffing

4 tablespoons butter
4 tablespoons chopped fresh herbs

Mash the butter and herbs together with a fork, then push between breast skin and flesh.

Mascarpone or cream cheese stuffing

Substitute 6 tablespoons mascarpone or cream cheese instead of the butter.

Lemon and garlic stuffing

1 lemon, halved
2 garlic cloves, crushed

One of the simplest stuffings. Put the lemon halves and garlic inside the cavity before roasting. Discard before serving.

Herb stuffing

Add a handful of fresh herbs, such as tarragon, parsley or thyme.

Trussing

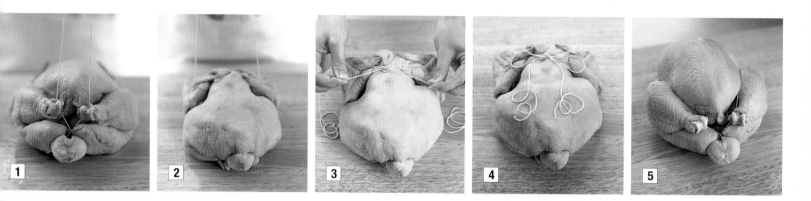

Chickens hold their shape and are easier to carve if you truss them. Very tight trussing (with string and using a trussing needle) may sometimes mean that the area between the breast and inner leg is undercooked. Check that ready-trussed birds do not contain giblets in the cavity.

String-trussing

1 To string-truss (without a needle): take a piece of string, 2 feet long, and tie it, criss-cross fashion, around the tail of the bird, then around, back up and over the legs, just in front of the knee joint. Leave it crossed, ends

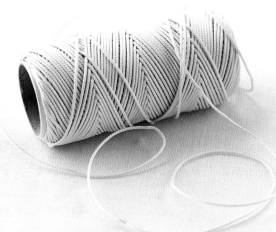

free. Cross the strings and pull them up either side of the breast between it and the legs.

2 Turn the bird over and thread the string around the innermost joint of the wings several times.

3 Pull the strings gently together.

4 Tie in a bow or knot.

5 Set breast up for cooking. Alternatively, it may be roasted breast down on one side of the breast, then the other. Another method is to cook it breast down on a V-shaped rack set in a roasting pan. Birds cooked breast down are regarded as moister and juicier.

Elastisized band truss

Oven-ready whole birds are sometimes sold ready-trussed with a cotton-covered elastisized band. However, this will leave the birds very loosely trussed.

Shortcut skewer truss

Set the bird breast up. Hold the legs tightly into the body, pushing them back and down firmly. Push a skewer through the flesh just below the knee joint, across into the side vent area and right through to the other leg and out.

Turn the bird over. Pull the neck skin (stuffed or not) over the neck cavity. Tuck the wing tips in to cover it. Skewer through both bent sections of one wing, through the neck skin, under the backbone and out to the other side, using the same technique.

To remove the wishbone

The French custom is to remove the wishbone, so it will be easier to carve the breast. It is optional, but if you choose to do so, it must be done before any stuffing or trussing.

Remember to keep the wishbone. It gets its name from the custom of drying the bone, then having two people pull it apart with their little fingers. The person who gets the larger part is allowed to make a wish.

Carving

My method of carving chickens is not the orthodox one. Usually, the legs and wings are removed first, then the breast is carved. However, I find that the bird becomes very unstable carved this way. Accordingly, I like to carve the breast first, then remove the legs, then the wings.

1 Hold the bird with a carving fork and cut slices off one side of the breast.

2 Repeat on the other side of the breast.

3 Insert the carving fork firmly into the chicken just above the inner leg, then cut down and through the joint.

4 Cut the leg in half at the knee joint, separating thigh and drumstick.

5 Insert the carving fork firmly into the breast and cut down and through the wing joint with the carving knife.

6 Arrange the chicken on a serving platter and serve.

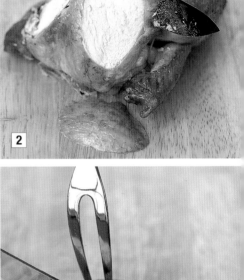

Chicken cooking temperatures

Chicken is perhaps the most popular of all meats, but also, together with fish, the most delicate. It is important that chicken be cooked right through and to the correct temperature. If it is to be cooled and refrigerated, it should be done quickly so it spends as little time as possible in the temperature "danger zone." If the chicken is to be reheated, it should also be done quickly and reheat it thoroughly.

• It is important to cook all poultry, whether fresh, chilled, or defrosted, to the correct internal temperature to destroy any harmful micro-organisms, particularly salmonella.

• A whole frozen chicken must be completely thawed before cooking (see chart opposite). Remember to remove the giblets before cooking.

• I do not stuff the body cavity. I find it slows heat penetration and can make the cooking uneven, resulting in undercooked or raw areas. Instead, I stuff the neck cavity alone or cook the stuffing alongside the bird. However, if you do stuff the cavity, do so just before cooking and remove it when cooked. It will take longer for a stuffed chicken to reach the proper temperature.

• Put the bird into a heavy-bottom roasting pan, loosely trussed or untrussed. Cook in an oven preheated to 375°F, allowing 20 minutes for each pound of oven-ready weight plus, if liked, 10–20 minutes extra.

Note: If you truss it too tightly, the heat will be unable to reach the fleshiest internal areas. These may remain semi-cooked or even raw.

• In France, roasted chickens are often cooked breasts down on a V-shaped metal rack set inside a roasting pan. If you don't have a rack, cook the bird breast side down for one-third of the cooking time, then cook it with the other breast down for the second third of the cooking time. Turn the bird breast up for the last third of cooking time. Many cooks now prefer to roast birds breast down for succulence.

• A chicken is well cooked when it is golden, aromatic, slightly shrunken and when the slowest-to-heat part, such as the center thigh, has reached at least 160°F for at least two minutes. Use a meat thermometer and make sure it is not touching the bone. Do not remove the chicken from the oven—test it in its normal cooking position.

• Another easy test: when the drumstick is wiggled, the thigh bone feels loose and flexible, not tight.

• Alternatively, pierce the thickest part of the thigh with a metal skewer: the juices must be clear, not cloudy—golden not pink.

• Some poultry are sold with a simple thermometer embedded in the flesh. When the central button pops out, the bird should be cooked through. Thermometers may also be bought separately.

• After the correct temperature has been reached, leave the bird, covered, in the turned-off oven with the door ajar for 5–10 minutes to allow the flesh to rest before carving. Then remove it to a warm platter for carving.

• Use the same tests for larger pieces of chicken, but also test the interior for color—pink means raw.

Microwave cooking

It is impossible to specify microwave cooking times since their performance varies so widely.

• Allow 8–10 minutes on HIGH per pound for whole birds, then allow to stand for at least 5 minutes.

• Cook in a roasting bag, breast up or down, with the bag loosely tied.

• For whole poussins, allow 5 minutes on HIGH per bird, also using a roasting bag, loosely tied.

• Use the same tests for doneness but using a microwave thermometer.

• Color can be improved if the bird is rubbed with honey and soy sauce before cooking.

Reheating

Remember that the aim is to reheat, not cook the chicken, to moisten, rehydrate, and revive its flavor by good use of spices, stock, seasonings, herbs, cream, coconut milk, vegetable, or fruit juices or a combination of these.

Ideally, bone the chicken and cut into ½-inch cubes or 1-inch strips. Add 1 part chicken (use a cup as a convenient measurer) to 1–2 parts liquid. If using in soups, use 1 part chicken to 3 parts liquid. Bring the chicken and its liquid almost to a boil, reduce to a steady simmer, partially cover (to reduce evaporation), and reheat for about 10–12 minutes or until evenly hot. Do not reheat, re-use cold, or refreeze.

Alternatively, grind the cooked chicken, season, flavor, then bind with a thick béchamel sauce or mashed potatoes. Shape into croquettes, cakes, or fritters. Flour or crumb the surface, then deep-fry, sauté, or bake until very hot. Do not overcook. Serve promptly: do not reheat or freeze.

Freezing

Uncooked whole chickens

Wrap whole birds individually in foil and overwrap in freezer-proof plastic bags. Seal with twisting metal ties or plastic clips. Pack giblets in rigid containers or plastic freezer-proof bags. Keep livers separate.

Uncooked half chickens or portions

Shield protruding bones with foil, wrap individual pieces in foil and pack in freezer-proof plastic bags sealed with twisting metal ties or plastic clips.

Cooked chicken

Cool completely in the refrigerator. Double wrap in sealed freezer-proof plastic bags. Use within 2 months or sooner if strong flavorings were used.

To thaw

Thaw uncooked frozen chickens to room temperature before cooking. Never cook a bird in a frozen state. Thaw it in the refrigerator in its sealed bag on a covered plate. This takes longer, but room temperature is the danger zone: it is a perfect environment for the growth of dangerous micro-organisms. Alternatively, thaw the chicken in cold water in its sealed bag. Replace the water every few hours. Never let chicken blood drip on other foods in the refrigerator, in the sink, or on the kitchen counter.

Thawing times

Weight	In refrigerator	In cold water
3 lb.	24 hours	8 hours
3½ lb.	36 hours	11 hours
4½ lb.	42 hours	13 hours
6–8 lb.	2–2½ days	16–18 hours

• Put the bird in a sealed bag and thaw slowly in the refrigerator or in cold water.

• Thawing in a microwave is not considered ideal, even if it is to be cooked immediately. Thawing poultry using a microwave can lead to the development of hot spots, so be careful. Follow the manufacturer's instructions.

• Micro-organisms previously inactivated by freezing may multiply rapidly in one part of the thawed poultry before the next section has even begun to thaw. This is risky—if in doubt, defrost the slow way.

• If you must use a microwave for thawing chicken, here are some guidelines:

Whole chicken

6 minutes per pound on LOW. Remove any giblets when they are free: cook promptly.

Drumsticks, thighs or whole legs

4 minutes per pound on LOW set on a rack, then in cold water for 15 minutes in a sealed bag.

Wings

7 minutes per pound on LOW, then in cold water for 15 minutes in a sealed bag.

Hygiene

Buying fresh chicken

• Look for chicken that is fresh, pale yellow, moist, and firm, with no discoloration or smell.

• It should be properly chilled.

• Learn the terminology for various methods of raising chickens. (see page 136).

• Always buy from a reputable source. Buy birds whose lives have been relatively stress-free, raised in good conditions with good feed, room to exercise and with access to outside vegetation. There should be a humane system of slaughter and efficient, sanitary processing.

Buying frozen chicken

• Preferably, buy frozen chicken that has NOT been processed using the water immersion process—a known hygiene risk.

• Chickens should be frozen solid with no damage, discoloration, or freezer burn.

• Take frozen chickens home as quickly as possible, ideally packed into an insulated bag to prevent any thawing.

• Keep the freezer at 0°F or below.

• Keep the chicken, double wrapped for protection, for no longer than 12 months.

• Chicken stock should be frozen for no longer than 6 months.

Refrigerator and freezer know-how

• Invest in a fridge thermometer (the ideal temperature is 40°F) and a freezer thermometer (ideal temperature is 0°F).

• Do not overfill your fridge and freezer: cold air must be able to circulate.

• Check that the pliable door seals (fridge and freezer) are effective.

• Never cool food in the fridge or freezer: cool it first over ice or cold water, and only then refrigerate or freeze, appropriately covered.

• Keep cooked and fresh chicken apart with the fresh chicken on the lower part of the refrigerator so it cannot drip onto the cooked chicken and contaminate it.

• Refrigerate chilled chicken for no longer than 2 days, cooked pieces and whole birds for 3 days and casseroles for 2 days maximum.

The kitchen environment

• Buy a thermometer for deep-frying and another for the oven.

• Get a microwave probe-type thermometer to monitor the internal temperature when cooking in a microwave oven.

• In the kitchen, keep separate cutting boards and knives for cooked and raw chicken to avoid cross contamination.

• Pat the chicken dry using disposable paper towels rather than cloth kitchen towels.

• Scrub down kitchen surfaces with detergent and hot water to sterilize the area where chicken was prepared.

• Air dry wooden utensils to prevent cracks from developing. Bacteria are drawn to them.

• Wash and dry your hands thoroughly after handling raw chicken and before handling any other food.

Micro-organisms and health

Micro-organisms are virtually everywhere. Some are beneficial, some are harmless, and some can cause damage as in the case of food spoilage. Others such as salmonella, botulism, listeria, and campylobacter can cause serious illness and even create life-threatening situations.

Poultry which has "gone off" presents a real risk of food poisoning, but it is not always easy to identify. Be vigilant; select, handle, prepare, cook, and store chicken effectively following the guidelines given.

Index

Conversion charts

Weights and measures have been rounded up or down slightly to make measuring easier.

VOLUME EQUIVALENTS:

American	Metric	Imperial
1 teaspoon	5 ml	
1 tablespoon	15 ml	
¼ cup	60 ml	2 fl.oz.
⅓ cup	75 ml	2½ fl.oz.
½ cup	125 ml	4 fl.oz.
⅔ cup	150 ml	5 fl.oz. (¼ pint)
¾ cup	175 ml	6 fl.oz.
1 cup	250 ml	8 fl.oz.

WEIGHT EQUIVALENTS:

Imperial	Metric
1 oz.	25 g
2 oz.	50 g
3 oz.	75 g
4 oz.	125 g
5 oz.	150 g
6 oz.	175 g
7 oz.	200 g
8 oz. (½ lb.)	250 g
9 oz.	275 g
10 oz.	300 g
11 oz.	325 g
12 oz.	375 g
13 oz.	400 g
14 oz.	425 g
15 oz.	475 g
16 oz. (1 lb.)	500 g
2 lb.	1 kg

MEASUREMENTS:

Inches	Cm
¼ inch	5 mm
½ inch	1 cm
¾ inch	1.5 cm
1 inch	2.5 cm
2 inches	5 cm
3 inches	7 cm
4 inches	10 cm
5 inches	12 cm
6 inches	15 cm
7 inches	18 cm
8 inches	20 cm
9 inches	23 cm
10 inches	25 cm
11 inches	28 cm
12 inches	30 cm

OVEN TEMPERATURES:

110°C	(225°F)	Gas ¼
120°C	(250°F)	Gas ½
140°C	(275°F)	Gas 1
150°C	(300°F)	Gas 2
160°C	(325°F)	Gas 3
180°C	(350°F)	Gas 4
190°C	(375°F)	Gas 5
200°C	(400°F)	Gas 6
220°C	(425°F)	Gas 7
230°C	(450°F)	Gas 8
240°C	(475°F)	Gas 9